train
your
dog

train
your
dog

a weekly program
for a well-behaved dog

Jacqui O'Brien

BARRON'S

A QUARTO BOOK
Copyright © 1999 Quarto Inc.

First edition for the United States and Canada
published exclusively 1999 by Barron's Educational
Series, Inc.

All inquiries should be addressed to:
Barron's Educational Series, Inc.
250 Wireless Boulevard
Hauppauge, NY 11788

http://www.barronseduc.com

International Standard Book No. 0-7641-0967-7
Library of Congress Catalog Card No. 98-40694

Library of Congress Cataloging-in-Publication Data
O'Brien, Jacqui.
Train your dog / Jacqui O'Brien. —1st ed.
p. cm.
ISBN 0-7641-0967-7
1. Dogs — Training. I. Title.
SF431.03 1999   98-40694
636.7'088'7-dc21   CIP

This book was designed and produced by
Quarto Publishing plc
6 Blundell St
London N7 9BH

Senior art editor **Penny Cobb**
Designer **Michelle Stamp**
Photographer **Paul Forrester**
Senior editors **Anna Watson**, **Sally MacEachern**
Text editor **Constance Novis**
Indexer **Dorothy Frame**
Art director **Moira Clinch**

QUAR.SIT

Manufactured in Singapore
by Bright Arts (Singapore) Pte Ltd
Printed in China by Leefung-Asco Printers Ltd

contents

introduction

This book is designed to make owning a dog rewarding and enjoyable. It will help you to communicate with your dog and to get to know your dog from the first day that it arrives in your home, whether as a puppy or as an adult. You need to learn to understand your animal's behavior in order to discover ways to teach it effectively.

There are four main sections in this book; the first three are devoted to training and development. Through play and incentives, you and your dog can move together from basic skills to more complicated exercises, gradually developing both the animal's concentration and your control. Each section includes aspects of care, handling, and grooming. These activities bring you and your dog together and build up the mutual trust, which is so essential for training. The fourth section looks at some common behavioral problems and how best to solve them.

It takes time to teach your dog how to fit into your way of life, but it will be time well spent. It is very satisfying when your dog responds to training and becomes an obedient and happy member of the family. As part of this process, your family's behavior, which will influence a dog's reactions, may need to be modified to prevent unwanted habits from being inadvertently taught. Remember that it is always easier to prevent a problem than cure it.

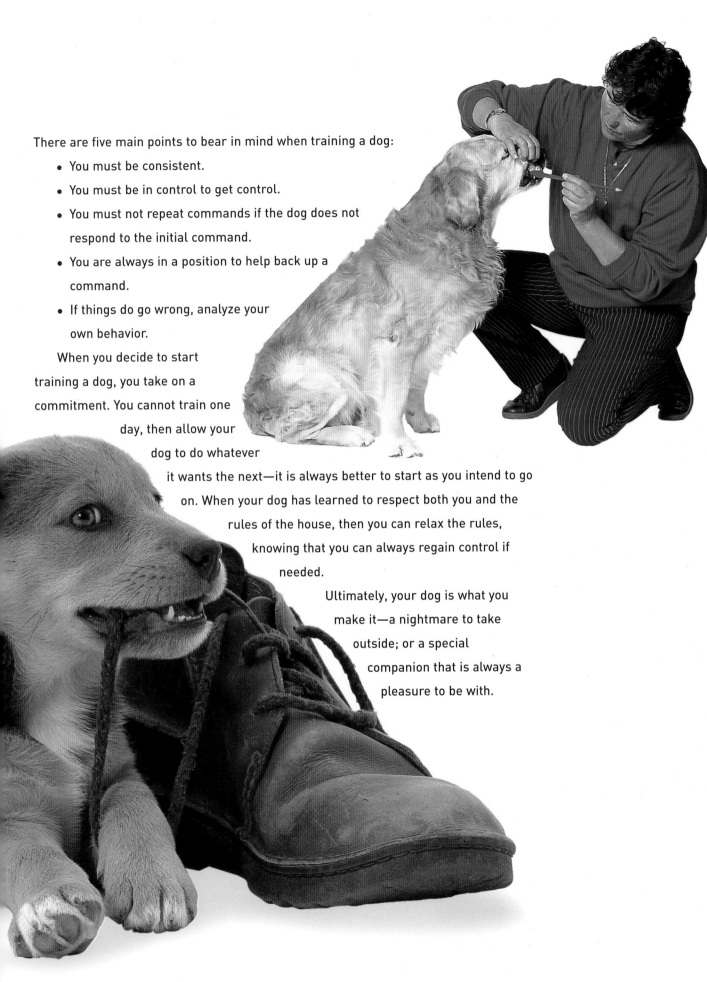

There are five main points to bear in mind when training a dog:

- You must be consistent.
- You must be in control to get control.
- You must not repeat commands if the dog does not respond to the initial command.
- You are always in a position to help back up a command.
- If things do go wrong, analyze your own behavior.

When you decide to start training a dog, you take on a commitment. You cannot train one day, then allow your dog to do whatever it wants the next—it is always better to start as you intend to go on. When your dog has learned to respect both you and the rules of the house, then you can relax the rules, knowing that you can always regain control if needed.

Ultimately, your dog is what you make it—a nightmare to take outside; or a special companion that is always a pleasure to be with.

how to use
the book and
progress chart

This book covers three training levels:

● **Foundation training** gives a thorough grounding, developing your handling skills and your dog's confidence in you. Training should be a daily, ongoing job—not just five minutes here and there. Success in foundation training means that more advanced training will go smoothly and that your dog will be less likely to develop behavioral problems. It will take 10 to 12 weeks to complete.

● **Basic training** builds on your early success, teaching your dog good manners at home and in public. You need to obtain gold medal status in each exercise to progress to advanced training. This should take approximately six months.

● **Advanced training** develops your partnership with your dog. It should take approximately six months.

Within each level, the order of exercises is not important—if you and your dog quickly obtain gold in one exercise, then move on to the next level.

If you need to use the problem-solving section, you will also need to refer back to relevant training exercises.

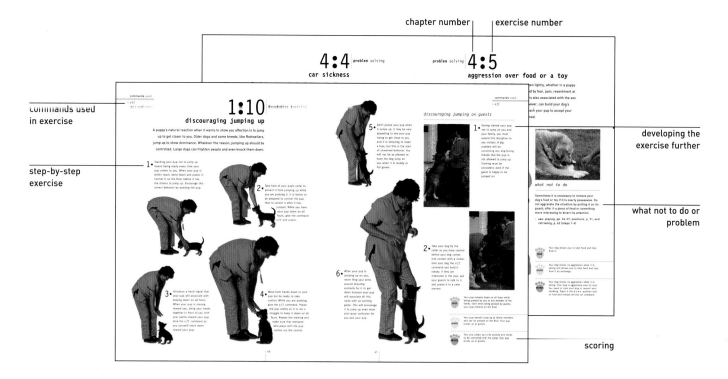

chapter number — exercise number

commands used in exercise

step-by-step exercise

commands used

developing the exercise further

what not to do or problem

scoring

progress chart

To assess your dog's progress, reward successes with a medal and point scores to give a weekly total.

Gold medal: 3 points

Silver medal: 2 points

Bronze medal: 1 point

At the end of each month, add up the weekly points and check them against the scoring levels (see right).

Throughout training there will be learning highs and lows. Always be ready to reteach an exercise or part of an exercise to help your dog overcome a difficulty. Always keep calm—if you feel like you are "losing your cool" stop training. If you or your dog are feeling under the weather, don't train.

If you need to use the problem-solving section, the chart will help you to keep track of your progress. Once you have achieved a gold medal, the problem should be solved.

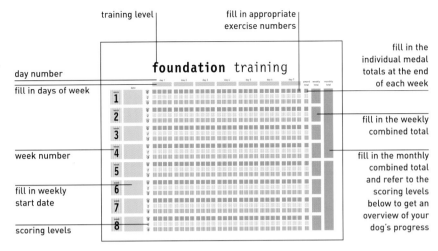

scoring levels

40 points or less means you need to give more time to the exercises because your dog is not responding as it should. **60–80 points** means your dog is trying hard and managing to learn, but needs more practice. **80 points or more** means you and your dog are doing well and making good progress.

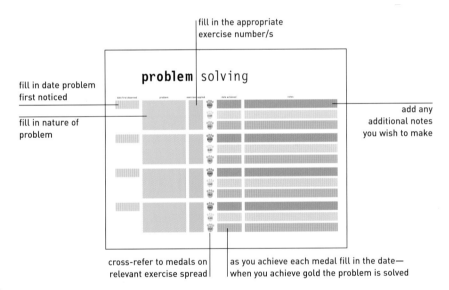

training score card

If you don't want to fill in the progress chart on a daily basis, turn to page 125, where we have included a training score card template. You can photocopy this as many times as required and use it to keep a record of exercises and achievements. You can also use it to supplement the progress chart once you have completed the course.

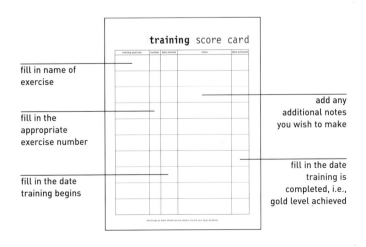

choosing an adult or a puppy

Do you choose an adult dog or a puppy? It's a big decision, and there are advantages and disadvantages to both. There are some other points to be considered in making the right choice, because you hope to live happily together for the best part of 10 to 15 years. Are you going to get a purebred or

a selection of popular breeds

Hunting breeds are bred to work closely with people. Spaniels and Retrievers have gentle natures, making them good family dogs. Setters and Pointers are more independent and have a tendency to range, which means they may not be ideal for first-time dog owners.

English Springer Spaniel

20 inches (50.8 cm)

26 inches (66 cm)

English Pointer

22 inches (55.9 cm)

Labrador Retriever

25 inches (63.5 cm)

Irish Setter

mixed-breed, male or female, large or small dog, long-coated or short-coated? The choice will depend on the reasons you want a dog and the environment in which it will be raised and live. With the wide variety of dog breeds available, you can almost have one tailor-made to fit your requirements.

Once you have decided on a breed that you like, visit a breeder or go to a show. At a show you will be able to see several examples of the breed and be able to talk to owners and breeders. Find out what the breed is like to live with and

if that type of dog would fit into your family, lifestyle, and routine.

If you decide that you wish to buy a puppy, contact a breeder. Go and see the puppies at about 4 to 6 weeks of age to make an initial selection before you make a final choice. View the mother and puppies, and, if possible, the father. This should indicate what your pup will look

The mother dog calmly gives her puppies the care and comfort they need at this early stage of their development.

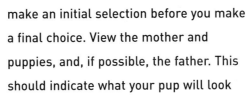

Terriers are tenacious, have a bold and fearless nature, are highly inquisitive, and have quick-snapping jaws. They can be independent and stubborn and need to learn to respect their owners through positive training and control. Many require specialist grooming to keep them in good shape. Cairn and Border Terriers make good family dogs.

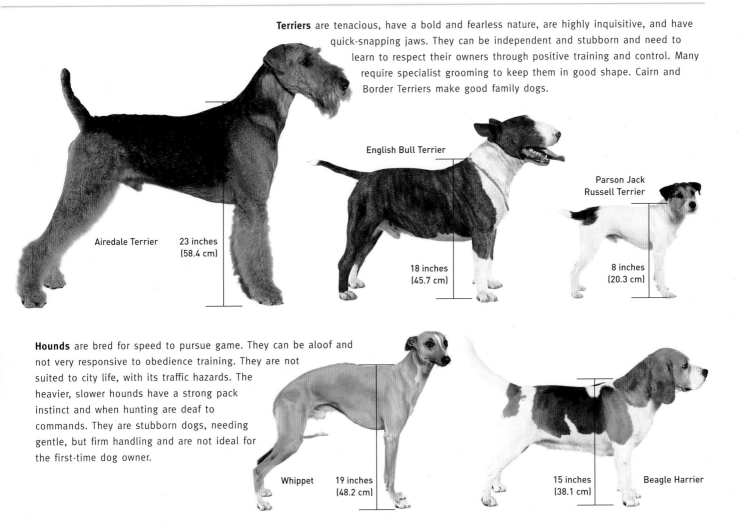

English Bull Terrier

Parson Jack Russell Terrier

Airedale Terrier 23 inches (58.4 cm)

18 inches (45.7 cm)

8 inches (20.3 cm)

Hounds are bred for speed to pursue game. They can be aloof and not very responsive to obedience training. They are not suited to city life, with its traffic hazards. The heavier, slower hounds have a strong pack instinct and when hunting are deaf to commands. They are stubborn dogs, needing gentle, but firm handling and are not ideal for the first-time dog owner.

Whippet 19 inches (48.2 cm)

15 inches (38.1 cm) Beagle Harrier

introduction

like when grown up and may also give you some clues as to its future character.

While you are there, note the living conditions, cleanliness, type of bedding, and material on the floor of the toilet area. Do the puppies have a play area with toys and apparatus to give them an opportunity to learn skills and familiarize themselves with various objects through communal play? Are they being given the opportunity to be handled and introduced to a normal household environment?

Handling is a very important part of a puppy's early education, and helps them get used to human company. Careful introduction of strangers and children is a good foundation for early social behavior and an easy nature. A well-adjusted puppy that is used to being handled will settle into its new environment and adapt to new experiences more easily.

For a family pet, it is best to choose a puppy that is neither the boss of the litter nor the one that sits nervously in the corner. Both of these extremes of character require experience and

Pup and adult dog playing together.

a selection of popular breeds

Working dogs are bred for a wide variety of tasks including pulling sleds, guarding property and livestock, heeling, and tracking.

Guarding breeds require careful socializing, supervision, and training from an early age. Many need to be mentally stimulated as well as physically exercised.

Herding dogs are bred to herd livestock and act as shepherd dogs. All are active, intelligent, and respond well to training. If they are not trained to accept moving objects, they can develop a desire to chase.

German Shepherd

24 inches
(61 cm)

Saint Bernard

29 inches+
(73.7 cm +)

Briard

25 inches
(63.5 cm)

Border Collie

21 inches
(53.3 cm)

understanding to help them develop into well-adjusted adults.

If you have decided to get an adult dog of a particular breed, contact a breeder because he or she may have an older pup or adult available. The breeder will also be able to put you in touch with his or her breed club, who will have full information about the breed, breeders, puppies, and older dogs needing homes.

You need to obtain as much background history on the dog as you can. As with a puppy, check out the dog's attitude and how it has been socialized.

Many adult dogs are well-adjusted animals that would make good pets and need new homes for no fault of their own. There are others, however, that need new homes because they are problem animals and may have major behavioral problems. Don't be taken in by those pathetic brown eyes looking appealingly at you through the bars of the kennel. Find out the facts before you make a commitment.

Rescue dogs may look very appealing, but don't be swayed by emotion. Find out about the dog before you offer it a home.

Toy dogs have been developed as small house dogs and companions. They do not see themselves as small, however, and can be very brave and can become very protective. Many respond well to gentle training, but are not ideal for a family with very young children, as they do not like rough handling.

Chihuahua

up to 6 lbs
(2.7 kg)

Pomeranian

4-5 lbs
(1.8-2.3 kg)

Toy Poodle

11 inches
(28 cm) max.

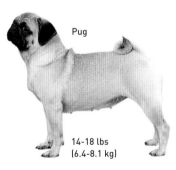

Pug

14-18 lbs
(6.4-8.1 kg)

Utility dogs have been bred for looks rather than working ability. They include independent dogs like Dalmatians and Chow Chows, Poodles who are very versatile and trainable, and Miniature Schnauzers, which are good city or country dogs. All of these dogs make good family pets.

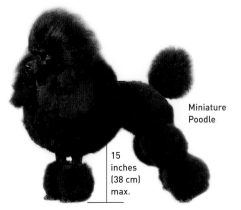

Miniature
Poodle

15
inches
(38 cm)
max.

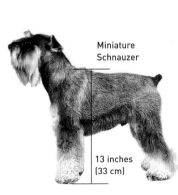

Miniature
Schnauzer

13 inches
(33 cm)

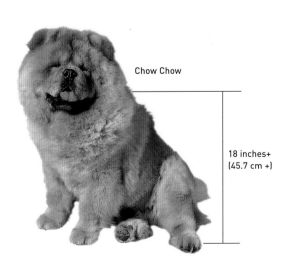

Chow Chow

18 inches+
(45.7 cm +)

communicating
with your dog

Effective communication is a two-way process. You expect your dog to understand you, but how much time and effort do you put into understanding your dog? Many difficulties experienced by dog owners come down to a fundamental lack of understanding. Reading your dog's body language, however, will enable you to preempt potential problems and prevent them from becoming bad habits.

the body language of dogs

Right A dog is honest and communicates its mood by the way it stands and by its expression. When it is feeling friendly toward another dog or a human, it wags its tail or its whole body. If the hairs on a dog's neck are raised, ears are laid back, teeth are bared, and it is growling, there is no mistaking its aggressive intent.

Above A confident or excited dog tries to make itself look tall. In such moods, the dog appears to be almost standing on its toes, with its ears up, and its tail high and slightly wagging.

Below A fearful dog or a dog that lacks confidence keeps itself low. The dog holds its head and tail low, holds its ears back close to its head, and almost seems to crouch.

Right The dog that wants to be playful holds itself in a "play bow" position. A dog that lowers its elbows to the ground and bows its front half low is asking for you (or another dog) to play with it.

Right A dog that is insecure or lacking in confidence will purposely place itself in its most vulnerable position when greeted to show that it is submissive. It will roll over on its back and will usually have its tail between its legs, its ears flattened, its eyes narrowed, and will often lick its lips. A dog that takes up this pose needs help to build up its confidence.

Above A dog wagging its tail is not always communicating that it is happy and friendly. A tail held stiffly straight up with a very short, fast wag is a warning that the dog is trying to exert dominance over another dog or is giving a human a warning to back off.

Left A dog's tail held level or slightly lower than its body is a neutral signal, usually indicating that the dog is feeling relaxed, secure, and friendly. The tail may be wagging in a slow, wide arc from side to side when nothing much is going on. When seeing a friend or its owner, however, the tail will vigorously wag at this level.

Left Dogs often misread friendly human intentions. Generally, people make eye contact, stretch out their hand, bend over a dog, and pet it. This makes a very imposing image, particularly to an insecure dog. It is best to get down to the dog's level, keep your arms and hands close to you, divert your face and eyes from the dog, and let it approach you.

Above An insecure, anxious, uncertain, and possibly fearful dog holds its tail low under its body, between its legs. If the dog wags its tail in this position it is a clear sign that the dog is worried about its situation. If confronted, a dog using this body language will often defend itself—only because it is frightened—by biting.

Right Dogs have to learn that affectionate gestures, such as petting the top of the head and down the neck and shoulders, are not threats. By cuddling a dog, you are not trying to dominate or intimidate it. It takes time, however, for a dog to learn that this kind of contact is a show of affection.

An important part of owning a dog is educating it. Your dog does not understand everything you say, although it may seem that way at times. Humans are creatures of habit and dogs are very observant. Dogs' ability to rapidly pick up on behavior patterns enables them to live with us. It can, however, prove to be a hit-and-miss process, so it is useful to look at ways of effectively communicating.

Consider the ways that you would set out to teach someone with learning difficulties. You would never shout or use threats to get through to them. You would break down ideas into easy steps and encourage any of their attempts at understanding. Likewise, you will have to take time and be patient to teach your newly acquired puppy. A puppy in a new home will have difficulties understanding your way of life and will be on a steep learning curve for the first few weeks as it tries to absorb every detail.

A dog's education must be based on the assumption that it does not reason and does not understand human language. A dog learns by associating our sounds, signals, and touch with a given action that is either encouraged or discouraged.

Below Your dog has no idea of what your words mean, but it listens to the sound of your voice. What matters is the tone and intonation that you use when speaking to it.

communicating with verbal cues

The tone of voice that you use is of the greatest importance throughout training. Use pleasant, encouraging, friendly, excited, cheerful tones to encourage the actions that you want to take place. Gruff, low, growly, sharp, annoyed tones should only be used for discouraging or stopping the actions that you do not want.

Right There should never be any need to shout. Dogs hear sounds over a longer distance and a wider range than humans. In particular, dogs with ears that stand up and breeds that can swivel and prick up their ear flaps have acute hearing. All breeds hear well enough that there should never be any need to raise your voice.

communicating with visual cues

Dogs mainly hunt at night in the wild, and have no need to distinguish colors. Dogs see better than we do in twilight and in darkness. They have a tendency to be farsighted and are able to see moving objects best. Training with visual commands will help give you control by creating a picture for your dog to follow.

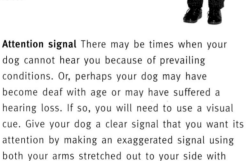

Attention signal There may be times when your dog cannot hear you because of prevailing conditions. Or, perhaps your dog may have become deaf with age or may have suffered a hearing loss. If so, you will need to use a visual cue. Give your dog a clear signal that you want its attention by making an exaggerated signal using both your arms stretched out to your side with your palms toward your dog.

Recall signal The *recall* signal is given with both hands together in front of you at approximately the height of your dog's muzzle. Encourage your dog to move close to you with a treat or by petting it. You are conditioning your dog to come close to your hand by associating this position with a reward.

Sit signal To give the *sit* signal, place the palm of your hand facing toward your dog while making an upward movement for your dog to watch. Because your dog will find it easier to sit and look up to watch your hand, it will automatically go into the *sit*.

communicating with physical contact

It is possible to train your dog without ever touching it. However, it is important that your dog learns to accept your handling and physical contact without feeling fear or the desire to escape. Sensitivity to touch varies between dogs. Some will need strong handling while others will respond to the lightest touch.

Training continues throughout a dog's entire life. When your dog becomes very old, its senses may no longer function as efficiently. Even if your dog cannot see or hear you, communication and control will still be possible through physical contact and touch.

Relaxing your dog The use of touch can help change and control your dog's emotions. Petting your dog gently but firmly on the head, cheeks, behind the ears, and along the side of the shoulders helps it relax. It also helps your dog associate pleasant feelings with being trained; it will then remain close to you.

Calming your dog To calm down your dog, place your hands on either side of its head with your fingertips between its jaw and ear; gently massage in a circular motion. Massaging along the dog's back muscles will also help to relax it.

Down signal When teaching your dog the *d o w n* command, first use your hand to get your dog to look toward the ground. This can be developed into a signal that can be used at a distance. When your dog sees you hold your hand flat with the palm toward the ground, making a clear downward movement, it will recognize the *d o w n* signal.

Stand signal To give the *s t a n d* signal, move your right hand from in front of you out to your right at about hip level. When teaching your dog to change position from the *s i t* and *d o w n* into the *s t a n d*, you encourage it to follow the hand movement and bring its weight forward so it can move its backside into the *s t a n d*.

Heel signal Placing your left hand against your left leg is the signal for the *h e e l* position. Give a light tap on your leg to get your dog's attention. The tapping movement and the position of your hand will become the visual reminder associated with the *h e e l* position.

Stop signal An instant *s t o p* signal involves moving your hand toward your dog while making a lunging step and body movement toward it. This acts almost as a shock and can be used to stop your dog immediately if its safety is threatened.

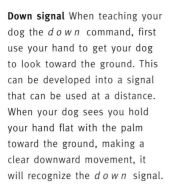

Exciting your dog To excite your dog, make quick, short strokes up and down against the fur around the dog's neck and shoulders. This is also a good way to initiate a game.

Sit hand contact While your pup is still learning, you can help place it in the *s i t* using physical contact. Stroke its backside and the root of its tail. Tuck its backside into the *s i t*. Do not exert any pressure on its hips. Eventually, it will understand that your hand on its backside means *s i t*.

Down hand contact Your dog can learn that your hand on its withers (the ridge between its shoulder bones) means *d o w n*. You can also assist your dog into the *d o w n*, if needed, by placing your finger and thumb around its neck. This will also prevent you from putting pressure anywhere else along its spine.

Stand hand contact Use your left hand to stroke along the pup's flank to its left knee. Prevent the pup from walking away, but do not put any upward pressure on the dog's abdomen. By touching and physically guiding the pup, use its natural movement to put it in the *s t a n d*, but do not use force.

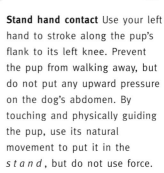

it's not what you do but the way you do it

The correct way to give a command:

- Use reassuring, positive tones to encourage your dog to perform an action.
- Keep a consistent tone, even when repeating the command.

The correct way to give a signal:

- Attract your dog's attention to ensure that it watches your movements.
- Keep your actions consistent and recognizable.

The correct way to use physical contact:

- Always use your dog's natural body movement as a guide.
- Never grab your dog or force it into a position.

praise and reward

Achievements, however small, and signs of progress are enhanced with the use of encouragement in the form of:

- a smile and praise given in a friendly tone;
- making a fuss by physically stroking and petting your dog;
- playing a game;
- giving food, such as a treat.

When your dog correctly responds to a verbal, visual, or physical cue, any or all of the above make appropriate praise and rewards.

physical rewards

A suitable reward depends on the temperament and attitude of your dog and what it is being taught at the time. Reward and praise your dog in a way that encourages it to continue with the exercise. This way, it will associate rewards with performing an action, not just completing it.

food rewards

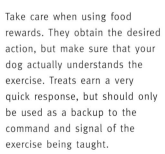

The treat should be very tempting and small. If it takes longer than two seconds to eat, your dog will forget why it was given the treat. Hold the treat between your finger and thumb to regulate when your dog can have the treat.

Take care when using food rewards. They obtain the desired action, but make sure that your dog actually understands the exercise. Treats earn a very quick response, but should only be used as a backup to the command and signal of the exercise being taught.

toy or play rewards

Right If your dog enjoys playing with you, a toy can be a useful training incentive. It focuses your dog's attention onto you and gives your dog an understandable reason for paying attention. Toys used during training should be kept separate from your dog's other toys.

Left Happy, confident dogs naturally play throughout their lives and even many older dogs can be stimulated by play. The effectiveness of playing games during training and its usefulness for diverting attention away from distractions should not be underestimated.

Below There is a wide range of good, safe toys on the market that are suitable for dogs of all shapes, sizes, and age groups.

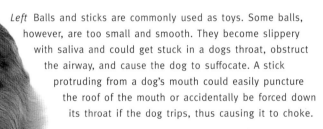

Right For a dog that enjoys running and chasing, a large rubber ring is ideal. It is easy to throw, has no sharp edges, and it cannot get stuck in a dog's throat.

Left A toy that floats provides good exercise for an older dog that enjoys swimming. A ball on a rope is safe to retrieve and can also be used for a good game of tug.

Left A dog that prefers tugging, seeking, and fetching will appreciate getting its teeth into a large knotted rope.

Left Balls and sticks are commonly used as toys. Some balls, however, are too small and smooth. They become slippery with saliva and could get stuck in a dogs throat, obstruct the airway, and cause the dog to suffocate. A stick protruding from a dog's mouth could easily puncture the roof of the mouth or accidentally be forced down its throat if the dog trips, thus causing it to choke.

timing

Timing is critical if your dog is going to understand and learn. No matter how clearly and consistently commands and signals are given, they will be meaningless unless they are timed in association with the action that you want the dog to perform.

foundation

You and your new puppy or dog need to learn the important fundamentals of training, get to know each other, and develop a sense of mutual trust and confidence. This includes teaching your dog to accept your handling and to respect your control. By doing this, you will be able to prevent any unwanted actions from becoming bad habits. The exercises in this section need to be undertaken every day. A lot of patience will be needed; always remember you are teaching your puppy and you may have to repeat certain exercises. Your aim at all times is to have a well-balanced puppy or dog that you can control in and around the home with your family and guests.

training

picking up your pup

Leaving its mother and siblings is a big occasion for the puppy, so when you pick it up ask someone to drive you. That way, you can comfort the pup on the way home. Ask the breeder for a piece of the pup's bedding or a toy, so it has something familiar in its new home.

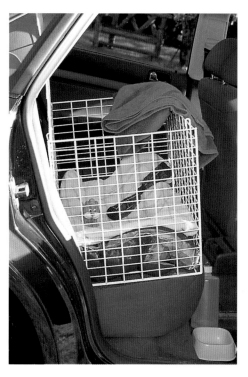

2. Do everything possible to make your pup's first journey a pleasant experience. If it is anxious, try to pacify it, or hold it on your lap. If it needs a drink, offer it a washcloth soaked in water to chew or suck instead of a bowl of water.

1. Place a box or pet carrier securely next to you in a draft-free position, with the pup's bedding in it. Place it so the pup cannot see out of the window; the traffic noise and movement could be very frightening. Have a towel or absorbent paper available in case it messes or vomits.

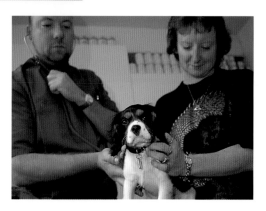

3. Your veterinarian should check the puppy before you purchase it. If this is not possible, make an appointment to see the veterinarian when you pick up your pup or very soon after. This way they can get to know each other and the pup's first visit will be a purely social one.

4. A good veterinarian will thoroughly examine your puppy in a relaxed, reassuring atmosphere. Do not delay taking your pup to the veterinarian until it is vaccination time. The injection may teach your pup to associate the veterinarian with pain and it will be frightened on future visits.

commands used

toilet
Use an encouraging tone that is not too loud or excited.

foundation training

1:2
housebreaking

Housebreaking starts as soon as you get your puppy home, in a quiet, nonthreatening manner. Take your pup to its toilet area on waking, after eating or playing, and before being left alone. It will perform on some of these occasions, giving you the opportunity to praise it and helping it to associate your command with going to the toilet.

1• The pup's toilet area, usually a dirt tray, in the house should be situated close to a door that leads outside. At any sign that the pup is about to relieve itself, such as sniffing or turning in a small circle, quickly pick up your pup and put it onto the dirt tray or, if there is time, take it outside.

2• When the pup has learned to use the dirt tray, move it outside but allow the pup access. If the door is closed, anticipate when it may want to go to the tray. Open the door, give the command *toilet,* and signal toward the dirt tray. Praise the puppy while it is performing, and repeat the command.

3• Gradually move the dirt tray closer to the area outside where you want the pup to relieve itself. Success depends on you anticipating your pup's need to urinate or defecate. Toilet training requires vigilance and perseverance, but it is a small price to pay to teach your puppy quickly.

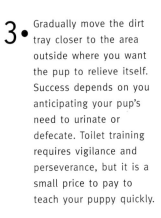

toilet training techniques

The choice of material for a toilet area depends on what was used as bedding material when the pup was with its litter. Enquire about this when you pick up your pup from the breeder. If it had paper bedding, then your pup will want to relieve itself onto anything other than paper.
• Do not let the pup out of your sight. If it is left alone, keep it in a small restricted area. It is important to pick up and dispose of the pup's feces. This eliminates the risk of the pup eating its own stool, possibly reinfecting itself with worms. Always clean up after your dog. Nothing causes more anti-dog feeling than dog dirt in public places.

 GOLD Your puppy does not relieve itself inside the house during the day or at night. Your puppy goes to the toilet outdoors and will go to the designated area on command.

 SILVER Your puppy does not relieve itself inside the house during the day and relieves itself on paper or on a dirt tray outside. Your puppy occasionally requires the indoor toilet area at night.

 BRONZE Your puppy relieves itself in the house, not always using the designated toilet area.

• *what's this?*
Use an excited tone
of voice.

1:3 | foundation training
playing

Play is an important part of a pup's development. It brings you together
and teaches the pup to respect you through play—sometimes the dog will
have to concede that you "win." Puppies deprived of play often show
behavioral problems later. Dogs of all ages enjoy playing and this
characteristic is a useful training incentive. Use toys that are unlike any
other household articles so it does not become confused between them.

1. Get down onto the floor to play. Have a gentle
game of tug using a toy that you can both
hold. If a pup is dominant, make sure that it
doesn't win. After playing with toys and having
had plenty of time to play, a puppy will be
more inclined to settle when left alone.

2. Playing in certain ways enables you to analyze your
pup's character. When you roll it over onto its back
is it submissive, staying there without biting or
objecting? Or does it fight to get up and prove
that it is
independent and
that it doesn't
like to be bossed
around?

3. Do not tug too hard on your pup's teeth. Move the toy around, saying *"What's this?"* Encourage the pup to follow and take hold of the toy. If the pup gives in too easily, let it win to build up its confidence. If it has a moderate temperament, alternate between letting it win and letting you take the toy.

4. To take the toy from your pup, reduce your pull, place a hand under its jaw, and put your fingers between its lips. When your pup drops the toy into your hand, praise it quietly. With a dominant, possessive pup that pulls hard and growls, stop the game before it becomes a battle of wills.

safe & unsafe toys

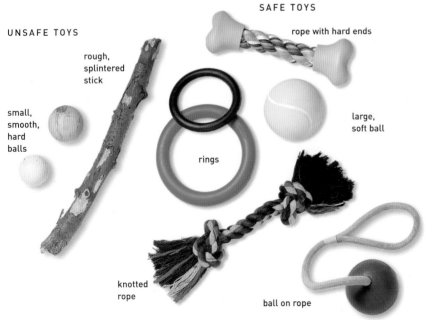

UNSAFE TOYS

rough, splintered stick

small, smooth, hard balls

SAFE TOYS

rope with hard ends

large, soft ball

rings

knotted rope

ball on rope

GOLD Your pup will play with various toys, following and taking hold of them. Your pup allows you to take a toy back. Your pup plays with other family members and allows them to take toys back. Your pup rolls over onto its back and allows you to play with it.

SILVER Your pup allows you to play with it and lets you take back the toy. Your pup plays with other members of the family but won't allow them to take back the toy. Your pup rolls onto its back for you but objects if other members of the family try it.

BRONZE Your pup shows little interest in playing. When it does play, your pup won't let you or any family member take its toys. Your pup rolls on its back to play.

responding to its own name

Name your puppy as soon as possible. Use the pup's name at every opportunity—when you are praising, playing, feeding, or teaching it the attention signal. It is important to get the name into your pup's mind. Use a short, crisp name, or one that has a friendly sound. The use of your pup's name is the only form of communication that can be changed with the circumstances and your mood without confusing the dog.

1. When the dog is well behaved, use a soft and gentle tone to say its name. Use another tone when it is misbehaving, and another when you are playing. Alter the tone of the dog's name depending on what is distracting it.

2. The pup's name should be used as an attention signal only—don't keep repeating it. Give it in the tone you know is going to get a response. Never give a command until you have your pup's attention. Your pup's training successes will depend on your ability to use your tone of voice to get its attention.

GOLD Your pup stops playing and looks at you when you call its name once. Your pup responds to its name when any member of the family calls it.

SILVER You have to call your pup's name a second time to attract its attention. Your pup is slow to respond to other members of the family.

BRONZE You have to repeat your pup's name several times before it pays attention.

1:5
positions

commands used

• *ss Sit*
Lengthen the "s" sound, using a light and slightly upward tone.

An essential part of your puppy's education is accepting your control and handling and learning to recognize various signals as commands. It is important during the learning phase that you encourage your pup's natural movement and never force it. Commands should be clear and distinctive and given when your pup is in position.

sit

The *sit* command gives you control over your pup's behavior when you are greeting visitors, grooming your pup, or putting on its collar and leash.

1• Position your pup by your left leg. Hold its collar with your right hand, using your left hand to stroke and assist your pup. As it relaxes, stroke down its back to its rump. Do not apply any downward pressure on its hips. Talk quietly to reassure it but do not give the *sit* command.

2• Continue stroking toward the root of the pup's tail and under its bottom. Tuck the pup into the *sit*, gently pulling the collar backward slightly. Quietly praise the pup to reassure it. If your pup gets up or squirms, calmly repeat the handling. Remember that the pup is learning.

3• As your pup takes up the *sit*, give the command and praise your pup by name in a friendly, calm tone. If the pup gets up, repeat the handling and command with the same tone and volume. Do not raise your voice. The pup is not being disobedient, it is trying to learn.

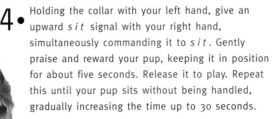

4• Holding the collar with your left hand, give an upward *sit* signal with your right hand, simultaneously commanding it to *sit*. Gently praise and reward your pup, keeping it in position for about five seconds. Release it to play. Repeat this until your pup sits without being handled, gradually increasing the time up to 30 seconds.

- *sit*
- *aaAND*
Lengthen the "a" sound, giving it a slightly nasal intonation. The "st" is dropped to distinguish this command from the *sit* command.

stand

The *stand* command gives you control over the dog during grooming and examination and is used in the show ring.

1. Start your pup off in the *sit* by your left leg. Hold your pup's collar with your right hand, using your left hand to stroke along its flank toward the abdomen. Talk quietly to the pup to reassure it.

2. As you reach the abdomen, take a step forward with your right foot. This helps bring your pup's weight forward, making it easier for it to rise. If your pup is slow to move, don't put physical pressure on it. Take another pace forward and encourage the pup. Do not command at this stage.

3. Keep hold of the collar to steady your pup. Use your left hand to stroke along the pup's flank to its left knee to help keep the pup in position. Give the *aaAND* command and quietly praise it. While your pup is learning, give the command only when it is in position and not before.

4. Now hold the collar with your left hand and use your right hand to give the *stand* signal, simultaneously saying the *aaAND* command. Keep your pup in the *stand* for about five seconds. Praise it and release it to play. Repeat this until it takes up the *stand* without manipulation.

down

The **d o w n** command gives you control over your dog during grooming and examination and teaches the dog to submit. It is also useful for keeping the pup still for any length of time.

commands used

- *s i t*
- *d o w n*
  Lower the tone of your voice and lengthen the sound of the word.

1• Place your pup in the *s i t* by your left leg. Place the palm of your left hand on its withers, holding its collar with your fingers. Use a treat to focus your pup's attention onto your right hand just in front of its nose.

2• The pup will follow the treat with its eyes as you lower it to the ground just in front of its feet. This hand movement forms the start of the *d o w n* hand signal. Keep your left hand on its withers without placing any physical pressure on the pup or giving a command at this stage.

3• As your pup looks toward the floor, move your hand a few inches forward so it has to lower itself toward the treat. Only when you feel your pup going into the *d o w n* should you help guide it with your left hand on the withers. Give the *d o w n* command and calm praise.

4• Keep your left hand on the withers to prevent your pup from moving. Use your right hand to give the *d o w n* signal, simultaneously giving the *d o w n* command. Keep your pup in position for about five seconds and then release it to play. Repeat this, gradually increasing the time.

GOLD Your pup takes up the *s i t*, *s t a n d*, and *d o w n* on your command and signal and remains steady while you praise and reward. It waits until you release it from position.

SILVER Your pup goes into the *s i t* and *d o w n* on your command and signal. It remains in *s i t* until you release it. Your pup gets up before being released from the *d o w n*. Your pup has to be helped into the *s t a n d*.

BRONZE Your pup goes into the *s i t* on your command and signal but moves before you release it. Your pup needs help to go into the *d o w n* and *s t a n d*.

31

1:6

grooming

Your puppy should be groomed every day to keep it healthy and presentable. Grooming is an ideal way to handle your pup and examine its condition. Grooming massages the skin, which stimulates the blood supply and improves the tone of the underlying muscles. It is better to spend five minutes a day brushing your pup than leaving it until the coat is tangled. Otherwise, grooming will take hours, causing the dog discomfort and pain, and discouraging it from being cooperative.

2• Place your pup in the *sit* to examine its eyes, ears, nose, and mouth and to clean its teeth. The teeth should be cleaned at least three times a week, if not every day. Choose a time of day that your pup is in a calm, quiet mood.

1• Choose a time of day when your pup is not excitable. Place it in the *sit*, so you can brush and comb the chest, behind the ears, and the front legs. If it is necessary to keep your pup still, hold its collar and reassure it with quiet praise.

3• Place your pup in the *stand* and use your fingers to feel behind its ears, along its flanks, and down its back to the tip of the tail. Feel for any tangles or skin blemishes that may need attention. Then comb and brush the pup thoroughly, not forgetting the backside.

4. Examine the pup's backside and the area under its tail while it is in the *stand*. Check that the area is clean. You can use a towel to clean your pup's legs and feet. If your pup thinks this is a game, keep calm and stop before your pup gets excited.

5. Put your pup into the *down* and reassure and relax it. Ease it onto its side so you can comb and brush its underside. You may have to spend several short sessions during the day to complete your pup's grooming. Always stop if it looks as if your pup is about to turn it into a game.

grooming equipment

6. Feel down the pup's legs and let it get used to having its feet touched. Examine its nails and check if they need to be trimmed. While your pup is in the *down* you will be able to examine its genital area. If necessary, divert its attention from the brush or comb with a toy or treat.

wipes
(for around eyes and ears)

chamois sponge
(for cleaning smooth-coated breeds)

soft brush
(for a puppy)

rubber brush
(for areas of short fur)

nail clippers
(for keeping nails short)

glove brush
(for final touches)

combs
(for getting right down into fur)

wire brush
(for all-over use)

toothbrush and paste
(for keeping teeth clean and breath sweet)

 GOLD Your pup keeps still while you examine and groom it all over. It allows you to clean its teeth and examine its feet.

 SILVER Your pup sits and lies down while you comb and brush it. It allows you to clean its teeth. Your pup will not allow you to examine its feet. Your pup will not remain in the *stand* while you examine and brush its backside.

 BRONZE Your pup plays with the brush and comb. Your pup won't allow you to examine or clean its teeth. Your pup takes up the *stand* but won't keep still while you clean its feet.

getting used to collar & leash

The collar and leash are important means of control, allowing you to adopt a natural position when training the dog or pup. The collar should carry the dog's identification. Leash training is an essential part of your dog's education, not just for walking but when teaching many exercises.

collar and leash made of soft, light material and with a snap

1. The pup's collar should fit snuggly and be made of a light, soft material, with a small buckle fixing. It will need changing several times until the pup is fully grown. Call your pup to you, then praise and make a fuss of it while putting on the collar.

2. It is not unusual for a pup to scratch the first time the collar is on. Divert its attention, have a game ready, or give it something to play with. If the pup becomes irritated and is frantic, take off the collar. Repeat the procedure during the day, gradually increasing the time the collar is left on.

3. When your pup is unperturbed by the collar, use it to teach the pup to accept your control and respect your handling. Bring your hand into the collar, applying light pressure, quietly praising and reassuring the pup. If it starts to struggle, say nothing until it is still, then praise and release it.

4. The lead should be 5 feet (1.5 m) long, made from a material that is comfortable to hold and strong, but light enough for your pup, with a suitable size snap. Hold your pup's collar and let it sniff the leash. Holding the leash a little way away, click the snap so the pup gets used to the sight, smell, and sound.

5. Attach the leash and then, holding it close to the collar, apply pressure toward you. Praise again and let the pup drag the lead. Use an incentive to get it to follow you. Before it loses interest, or tries to run off, step on the leash and call your pup to you. Hold the collar; unclip the leash, praise then release.

6. Any new experience should be introduced with the least amount of upset. When the collar and leash are accepted, use them occasionally to walk your pup around the house and yard. To get your pup used to the restriction and staying close by your side, make it fun and give a reward while the leash is attached.

GOLD Your pup accepts the collar and wears it during the day. Your pup remains quiet when the leash is attached, with no jumping up. Your pup walks happily on the collar and leash around the house and yard.

SILVER Your pup accepts the collar and wears it during the day. When the leash is attached, your pup resents the restriction and jumps up.

BRONZE Your pup will not wear its collar all day and struggles against your control. When the leash is attached, your pup jumps up and tries to bite the leash. Your pup occasionally goes into the *sit* and refuses to walk.

● *c o m e*
Use an encouraging,
friendly tone.

1:8 foundation training

recalling the puppy to you

The recall is the most important exercise. It will give you peace of mind
because you will know that you can call your pup to you when it is
necessary. Never call your pup to you to scold it. Do not run after or grab
at a pup; this will only teach it to avoid getting caught.

1. Every time your pup comes to you, make a
fuss over it, using your hands to reward it.
(Being seated prevents you from chasing
your pup and brings you down to its level.)
While fussing, give the *c o m e* command to
condition your pup to associate the sound
with the pleasure of your hands on it.

2. Call your pup's name in an excited tone. As
soon as it looks at you, hold your arms and
hands out to the side to focus its attention
on you. Encourage it to move to you and
praise your pup when it reaches you. Repeat
the *c o m e* command and make a fuss over
your pup.

3. While you praise the pup
and make coming to you
a highlight, control your
pup by holding its collar.
This prevents it from
jumping all over you in its
excitement and also stops
it from running away
when it has had enough
attention. You remain in
control of its release.

4. Get your pup's attention by using its name
and placing your hands out to the side. Use
the *c o m e* command. As your pup moves
toward you, bring your hands together close
in front of your legs, level with the height
of your pup's nose. Focus its attention on
your hands.

5. Let your pup sniff your hands. Don't move toward your pup. If it is slow coming to your hands, go forward just enough to focus its attention on your hands. Then move back a couple of paces saying "*Come*" in an excited tone. As your pup moves close to you, praise and reward it.

6. Your pup should associate the movement of your hands into the greeting position as the *come* signal. Call your pup and place your hands in the greeting position. When your pup reaches your hands, lift them up a couple of inches to encourage your pup to look up.

7. Looking up at your hands causes your pup to sit because it shifts the pup's weight to its backside and the pup finds it easier to sit and look up. The instant it sits, praise and reward it and give the *sit* command in a friendly tone. Bend down, put your hands on the pup, and praise it.

GOLD — Your pup comes to your hands on command and takes up the *sit* to be praised and rewarded. Other members of the family can call the pup to them and it sits for them.

SILVER — Your pup comes to your hands. Your pup goes to other members of the family but doesn't sit.

BRONZE — Your pup is slow to come to your hands. Your pup stays just out of your reach.

1:9 foundation training

feedback

Your puppy needs to understand when it is doing something wrong and when it is being good. In addition, you need to be able to interpret your pup's response. Your tone of voice, your attitude, and your facial expressions will all have an influence on your dog.

1. Saying "*No!*" in an angry, gruff tone is a useful command when your pup misbehaves. Don't nag the pup by repeating it; just use it once. Your pup's ears will go back close to its head and it will lower its whole body, almost collapsing in a heap, because the pack leader is annoyed.

2. Your pup may come to you in low, crouching stance with its eyes half closed, tail low between its legs wagging nervously. The pup is feeling anxious and looking thoroughly remorseful. Do not make it feel any more insecure by nagging it.

3. Saying "*Good dog!*" in a friendly, excited tone enhances and encourages the behavior you want from your puppy. Use it when your pup is responding correctly to a command. Your pup will feel confident and wag its tail with excitement.

4. Your puppy will respond to your friendly tone by listening with its ears up and having a bright look in its eyes. It will look confidently toward you for your approval.

5. With all this encouragement, your pup will feel confident and respond by bouncing around. If, in its excitement, your pup jumps up at you, simply place your hands on its collar to control it. Don't scold it.

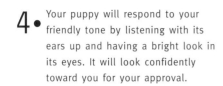

 GOLD Your pup stops any misbehaving the instant you say "*N o !*" Your pup looks remorseful, and comes to be comforted. Your pup responds to other members of the family. Your pup responds when you say "*G o o d d o g !*" by wagging its tail. It bounces around under control and does not jump up.

 SILVER You have to repeat "*N o !*" before your pup stops misbehaving. Your pup responds when you say "*G o o d   d o g !*" by wagging its tail and bouncing around under control.

 BRONZE You and your family have to repeat "*N o !*" before your pup stops misbehaving. Your pup gets excited and jumps up when you say "*G o o d   d o g !*"

1:10

discouraging jumping up

A puppy's natural reaction when it wants to show you affection is to jump up to get closer to you. Older dogs and some breeds, like Rottweilers, jump up to show dominance. Whatever the reason, jumping up should be controlled. Large dogs can frighten people and even knock them down.

1• Teaching your pup not to jump up means being ready every time your pup comes to you. When your pup is within reach, bend down and praise it. Control it on the floor before it has the chance to jump up. Encourage this correct behavior by praising the pup.

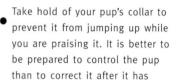

2• Take hold of your pup's collar to prevent it from jumping up while you are praising it. It is better to be prepared to control the pup than to correct it after it has jumped. While you have your pup down on all fours, give the command *off* and praise.

3• Introduce a hand signal that your pup will associate with staying down on all fours. When your pup is moving toward you, bring your hands together in front of you with your palms toward your pup. Give the *off* command as you yourself move down toward your pup.

4• Move both hands down to your pup but be ready to take control. While you are praising, give the *off* command. Praise the pup calmly so it is not a struggle to keep it down on all fours. Repeat the training and make sure that everyone who plays with the pup carries out the control.

5. Don't praise your pup when it jumps up. It may be very appealing to see your pup trying to get close to you and it is tempting to make a fuss, but this is the start of unwanted behavior. You will not be as pleased to have the dog jump on you when it is muddy or full grown.

6. When your pup is jumping up on you, never fling your arms around shouting excitedly for it to get down because your pup will associate all this noise with an exciting game. This will encourage it to jump up even more and cause confusion for you and your pup.

discouraging jumping on guests

1. Having trained your pup not to jump on you and your family, you must extend this discipline to any visitors. A big problem will be convincing any dog-loving friends that the pup is not allowed to jump up. Training must be consistent, even if the guest is happy to be jumped on.

2. Take your dog by the collar so you have control before your dog comes into contact with a visitor. Give your dog the *off* command and hold it steady. If they are interested in the pup, ask your guests to talk to it and praise it in a calm manner.

GOLD Your pup remains down on all fours while being praised by you or any member of the family. Even when being praised by guests, your pup remains on the floor.

SILVER Your pup doesn't jump up at family members and can be praised on the floor. Your pup jumps up at guests.

BRONZE Your pup jumps up to be praised and needs to be controlled with the collar. Your pup jumps up at guests.

commands used

- *h e e l*
- *s t o p*
  Use a hard, positive
  tone, emphasizing
  the "p."
- *g o o d   d o g !*

1:11 | foundation training

discouraging running through a gate or door

Teaching your puppy not to run through an open doorway could save its life and will certainly give you peace of mind. Any door that leads outside, including the car door, poses a potential danger.

1. Put your pup on its collar and leash and position it by your left side. Fold up the leash in your left hand to free up your right hand to open the gate. Walk forward toward the gate with your pup in the *h e e l* position. Do not allow your pup to pull forward.

2. When you reach the gate, use the leash in your left hand to hold back your pup. Give the *s t o p* command. At the same time, give a signal with your right hand, with your palm toward your pup's face. Do not give your pup a second chance. It must learn to stop in its tracks.

3. As you open the gate, give the *s t o p* command and hold back your pup, keeping it still. It does not matter what position the pup is in, as long as it gets used to stopping. Using a quiet, calm voice, praise the dog, saying "*G o o d   d o g !*" After a few seconds, walk the dog through the gateway.

4. As you open the car door or tailgate, give the *s t o p* command; don't let your dog jump out. Always attach its leash before allowing the dog to get out of the car. Keep the dog steady as you attach the leash. When your dog has been still for a few seconds, praise it calmly.

5. Encourage your dog to get out of the car by using its name and by signaling with your hand. Follow these procedures with any door in the pup's environment that leads to the outside world.

GOLD Your pup waits while the door is opened. You can walk your pup on its leash to the front door and it does not pull and waits until you encourage it through. Your pup waits in the car to have its leash put on.

SILVER Your pup waits in the car for its leash to be put on. Your pup waits at the back door to be let into the backyard. You have to repeat the *s t o p* command and hold your pup back at the front door.

BRONZE Your pup waits to be let out of the back door. Your pup pulls on its leash to get to the front door. You have to repeat the *s t o p* command and hold the pup tight as the door is opened. Your pup squirms to get out of the car before its leash is attached.

1:12
walking to heel

commands used

- *s i t*
- *h e e l*
  Use a friendly,
  encouraging tone.
- *c l e v e r   p u p p y*
- *o f f   y o u   g o*

A basic part of your puppy's training is learning to walk quietly under control on a leash reasonably close by your side. Conditioning your pup to walk to heel and associating your command in familiar surroundings around the house and yard will help build its confidence before you take it on its first outdoor walk.

2. Give the pup's name to get its attention, then the *h e e l* command in an encouraging tone. Tap your leg with the left hand as you step forward. Praise and encourage the pup, keeping it close to your side. Give the *h e e l* command only when the pup is in position.

3. When the pup has walked a few paces, stop and shorten the leash, keeping the pup close to your side. Praise with "*C l e v e r   p u p p y*" and repeat the *h e e l* command. Repeat the exercise until the pup is walking on a loose leash and paying attention to you. Always encourage your pup with a friendly tone.

1. Hold the leash and any excess in the right hand, with your arm bent across your body. Use the left hand for giving the signal and holding the leash to keep the pup in position, as and when necessary. Start with the pup in the *s i t* by your left leg.

Your pup does not get excited when the leash is attached to the collar. Your pup pays attention to its name, moves with you as you step forward, and stays by your side. Your pup stays quiet as the leash is taken off and waits for your signal and command to go and play.

GOLD

Your pup allows the leash to be attached to the collar. Your pup is slow to respond to its name; the leash needs to be used to keep it in position. Your pup doesn't remain still while the leash is taken off.

SILVER

Your pup jumps up as the leash is attached, is slow to respond to its name, and pulls the leash, making it difficult to walk. Your pup tries to struggle free when the leash is being taken off.

BRONZE

4. At the end of the session, walk the pup under control to a safe area of the yard. Place the pup in the *s i t*, hold the collar and unclip the leash. Don't let it struggle free. After a couple of seconds, give the release command "*O f f   y o u   g o*" to let it go and play.

commands used

- *what's this?*
- *fetch*
Use an encouraging, positive tone.

1:13 foundation training
retrieving

Puppies will pick up anything and everything, including things they shouldn't. To maintain this natural desire, it is important that you do not discourage them when they have something that they shouldn't; instead, exchange it for something that they can have. Condition your pup to bring to you whatever it picks up. Even when your pup comes to you with something that it shouldn't have, greet the pup and then take the article. Make this training into an enjoyable and exciting game by throwing different things for the pup to run after.

stage 1

1. Put a collar and leash on your pup. Choose an article that your pup will like and that you can both hold. Keep this article for training only and do not use one of its toys. Move the article along the ground a little distance in front so the dog can focus on it. Putting it just under the pup's nose will be too close.

2. Encourage your pup to take hold of the object by saying *"What's this?"* Once it has grabbed the toy, give praise and a gentle tug on the toy so the pup takes a better grip. Pull the article toward you. Repeat the *fetch* command so the pup associates it with having something in its mouth.

3. After a few seconds take the article. Place a hand under its jaw to get your pup to release it. Don't pull it out because your pup associates this with taking a grip. Repeat the above, and encourage your pup to your hand with a gentle pull on the article. Introduce various articles for the pup to retrieve.

stage 2

1. Take your pup off its leash. Get your pup to take hold of the retrieve article. When it has a good grip, let go immediately; turn and run a short distance away. This will make the pup chase after you and teaches your pup to move toward you.

2. As soon as your pup reaches you, take hold of the article, pull gently and praise. Give the *fetch* command and praise it. This teaches your pup that it is fun to bring the article to you and it also learns to associate the *fetch* command with gripping. Then take the article.

stage 3

1. Now teach your pup to run and retrieve something. Position your pup at your left leg with the article to be retrieved in your right hand. Walk forward with your pup by your left side. Tease it with the article and as soon as it wants it, throw the article. Let your pup chase after it.

2. Follow your pup, moving quietly up behind it. Do not give any command. As the pup picks up the article, stay close to discourage the pup from running away or standing by itself and playing with the article.

3. Take hold of the end of the article, pull it gently, and give the *fetch* command. Praise the pup and encourage it to move toward you using the *come* command. Make a habit of taking things out of your pup's mouth and not letting the pup drop things to the ground.

4. Before taking the article, repeat the *fetch* command as you stroke the top of the pup's muzzle. Praise the pup and then take the article. This early training is conditioning your pup to bring things to you. Your dog will enjoy this exercise as you are having fun together.

• *fetch*

start retrieve training with a knotted rope

stage 4

1. To teach the pup to wait until it is commanded to go and pick something up, place your pup on your left side, holding its collar to keep it close. Hold an article in your right hand and use it to get your pup's attention. Then, throw the article a few feet in front of you.

2. As you let go of your pup's collar, signal with your right hand for it to go forward. Give the *fetch* command, encouraging it to go and pick up the article. If your pup is slow, don't repeat the command or wave your arms around, but go quickly to the article and move it around.

3. Keeping quiet, follow closely behind your pup. Once your pup picks up the article, use its name to encourage it to turn to you. Praise the pup. If it is slow to return to your hands, move away. Do not make any grabbing movements toward your pup.

4. As soon as your pup makes contact, take hold of the end of the article, give a gentle pull, and give the *fetch* command after a few seconds. Praise the pup while the article is in its mouth and repeat the command, then take it.

GOLD — You can hold your pup by your side as you throw the retrieve article approximately 10 feet (3 m). Your pup goes to pick up the article on your command and signal, then brings it to your hand. Your pup picks up various articles that you throw and brings them back to you.

SILVER — Your pup goes forward to pick up the retrieve article, but needs you close by to have a game. Your pup is slow to pick up a variety of articles.

BRONZE — You have to encourage your pup to pick up an article by moving it along the ground. Your pup picks up articles and runs away.

46

1:14

traveling in the car

Your puppy needs to learn to be a good traveler. The first few journeys should be short and devoted entirely to the pup. Once they are accustomed to riding in cars, most dogs settle down and go to sleep on the seat. Your dog should feel secure and comfortable in the car and should not interfere with or disturb the driver.

harness

A harness is ideal to restrict an excitable young dog or to give better security to an old dog. It uses the car safety-belt system and allows the dog to sit on the backseat without interfering with the driver. A harness also prevents a dog from jumping out of the car.

grill or dog guard

Dog guards come in various designs, most commonly seen as grills. Fitted behind the backseats of station wagons, they prevent dogs from jumping or being thrown forward. Complete cage systems with grills are ideal for larger dogs or more than one dog.

carry box

Tiny puppies are best transported in a traveling box to prevent them from being thrown around. The box can be secured on the passenger seat for early training, close enough to be comforted. When the pup has grown accustomed to the confinement, move it to the backseat, but still within your reach.

GOLD
Your pup settles down in the car and doesn't bark or struggle to get to the driver.

SILVER
Your pup settles down after a while, but eventually tries to get attention.

BRONZE
Your pup tries to climb over the front seat to get to the driver or passenger. Your pup makes noise in the car.

basic

To progress to any of the exercises in this chapter, you need to have obtained gold medals at the previous level. You are now going to develop the foundation training of the previous chapter into everyday good manners in public. You need to be dedicated and consistent. Important aspects of developing your relationship and control will involve playing with your dog and utilizing its natural instincts. Don't forget that your dog is learning what you want it to do, so be ready to help and reteach. After you and your dog have worked through basic training, you should be able to control your dog in public and it should have the confidence to be left alone for short periods at home.

training

• *h e e l*
Use a friendly,
encouraging tone.

2:1 | **basic** training

heelwork

Training your dog to walk by your side under control will provide
excellent exercise for both of you. Once your dog has mastered walking
on a leash beside you, you can teach it how to change direction. You can
also help it learn the difference between formal and casual walking.

right circle: teaching the right and about turn

small,
squeaky
toy to help
keep your
dog's attention

1. Put your dog on its leash and position it by
your left leg. Bring the collar high on its
neck to just behind its ears. Hold the leash
and a toy in your right hand. Your left hand
should grasp the leash only when it is
necessary to keep your dog in position.

2. To teach your dog to stay
close when turning about
or right, walk in a circular
direction to the right. Call
the dog's name and praise
it when it looks at you.
Immediately give the
h e e l command, walking
forward. As soon as you
are close together, circle
to the right.

3. Travel in a circle of
approximately 5 feet
(1.5 m) in diameter. Hold
the toy close in front of
you and keep your dog
interested in it. Use your
movement and
encouraging vocal tones
to hold your dog's
attention. When the dog
is even with your left hip,
give the *h e e l* command.

4. Once you have made a
complete circle to the
right with your dog
happily keeping position,
take a straight line out
of the circle. Stop and
praise the dog by your
side. Gradually reduce the
size of the circle until you
and your dog can turn
right about.

left circle: teaching the left and left-about turns

1. Holding the leash and the toy in your right hand, get your dog's attention. Give the *heel* command and move forward. As soon as you are moving close together, bring your left hand down the leash toward the dog's collar. Keeping the dog close to you, circle to the left.

soft, light rope leash is ideal for teaching heelwork to older pups and dogs

2. Travel in a circle of approximately 5 feet (1.5 m) in diameter, keeping your left hand in position on the leash. Use the movement to the left to keep a close *heel* position. Hold the dog's attention with the toy and encouragement. Turning your upper body toward the left will help guide the dog.

3. Continue moving to the left in a circle. Directing your movement in toward your dog will help it hold its position. Changing pace will also keep its attention. Do not put any backward pressure on the collar. If the dog goes ahead, use a short leash and hold it close.

4. Once you have made a complete circle to the left with your dog easily keeping position, take a straight line out of the circle and stop. Praise the dog by your side. Gradually reduce the diameter of the circle until you can turn to the left keeping your dog close.

- *heel*
- *good dog/ dog's name!*
- *sit*

an adjustable double slip collar and adjustable leash is ideal for everyday use

informal walking on a leash

1• With the collar high on the dog's neck, hold the leash in the *heel* position to help control your dog. Walk forward, then change direction to the right. Using your left hand, encourage the dog to stay close. Use the *heel* command and verbal encouragement as the dog follows you.

2• Walk naturally. When the dog is walking beside you, teach it to be attentive with verbal encouragement such as *"Good dog! Heel!"* When the dog is in position, take your left hand off the leash. If the dog moves away, be ready to put your left hand back on the leash quickly.

3• About three paces before you change direction, attract your dog's attention by calling its name. Grasp the leash with your left hand in front of your left leg. When you have control, give the *heel* command. As you turn to the right, praise your dog for staying in position.

4• When approaching a road, get the dog under control by grasping the leash with your left hand and holding the dog close. About three to four paces before you intend to stop, attract your dog's attention by calling its name and giving the *heel* command.

5• Stop about three to four feet (1 to 1.2 m) away from the curb. All of your attention will now be on your dog. Approach the curb at a slow pace and use the leash to keep the dog close. Attract its attention as you stop by simultaneously commanding and signaling it to *sit*.

casual walking

1. At times, you and your dog may want to relax and take it easy while you are on a walk. After some control walking, stop your dog with the *sit* command. Use your left hand to loosen the dog's collar and reposition it lower on the dog's neck.

2. The dog will learn the meaning of the different collar positions. When the collar is high, the dog is under close control. A low collar represents the relaxed position. Hold the leash by the handle and allow the dog to move away.

3. Although you are about to allow your dog to move to the end of its leash, it is still under your control and must wait until you say it can go. To indicate that it has your permission, signal forward to your dog and say *"OK — off you go!"*

collar in high position for
close control

collar in low position for
casual and relaxed work

4. When you are out walking, your dog will inevitably find areas that it wants to investigate. Perhaps it is looking for something to play with, or just exploring its surroundings. Keep your attention on your dog. As long as the dog is under your control, you can allow it to investigate.

 GOLD — Your dog walks under control on a loose leash. Your dog changes direction, staying close by your side. Your dog sits at the curb. Your dog sits while you change the position of its collar and waits for your command to go forward to the end of the leash.

 SILVER — Your dog walks on a loose leash. Your dog needs your guidance using the leash to be able to change direction successfully. Your dog sits at the curb. Your dog moves away from you to investigate before you give it the command to go forward.

 BRONZE — Your dog pulls on the leash. You need to hold the leash with your left hand to keep your dog in position. Your dog pulls away to the end of the leash before you give your command.

- *sit*
- *stand*
- *down*

Use a firm but friendly tone.

2:2 positions

The *sit*, *stand*, and *down* positions teach your dog to obey your command and signal and to remain in a position until you release it. These positions are useful for improving control of your dog in everyday situations.

1. While out walking, you meet a friend. Use the leash to control your dog and keep it close by your side. Give the command and signal for your dog to take up the *sit* position. When giving the *sit* command, say "s s I T," emphasizing the end of the word. Training a dog to sit and remain still enables you to have an undisturbed conversation.

2. Train your dog to take up the *stand* position confidently and, once standing, to remain still for about one minute. If your dog is being weighed, encourage it to step onto the scale. Reassure it and then give the *stand* command and signal. When giving the *stand* command, start by saying "a a AND," omitting the "st," which the dog might confuse with the *sit* command. On completion, praise and congratulate the dog.

3. It is an advantage to be able to control your dog in a confined area or among other animals. First, allow your dog to relax. A mature, confident dog can be given the *down* command. A less confident dog should be kept closer to you and given the *sit* command. Repeat the command as necessary.

GOLD Your dog obeys the *sit*, *stand*, and *down* commands and remains in position until you praise and release it. Your dog obeys the *sit* command and remains still while you have a conversation. Your dog stands for 45 seconds, sits for one minute, and lies down for two minutes.

SILVER Your dog obeys the *sit* command and remains still for 45 seconds. Your dog obeys the *stand* command and remains still for 30 seconds. Your dog obeys the *down* command and remains still for two minutes. Even if you praise your dog, it still waits for a command to be released.

BRONZE Your dog takes up the positions on your command and signal. Your dog can sit for 30 seconds. Your dog can take up the *stand* position for 30 seconds. Your dog can stay in the *down* position for one-and-a-half minutes.

4. Group training teaches your dog to remain in position around other dogs. Always remember to praise your dog for remaining still.

2:3
playing

Playing games with your dog enhances its desire to be with you and helps distract it from potential problems. Scent games and games of hide-and-seek channel and hone your dog's natural instincts. Simply letting your dog go out by itself will make it independent of you.

developing attention

1. First, you must get your dog's attention. When there are no other distractions, calling a dog by its name is usually sufficient. As your dog matures, however, it will be distracted by other more interesting things. Entice your dog by choosing a toy that it loves to play with.

ball on a rope

large, soft ball

knotted rope

3. After a few seconds, throw the toy for your dog to fetch. Repeat the exercise. Gradually increase the time you keep your dog focused on the toy. This will develop its ability to concentrate. Throwing the toy in different directions teaches your dog to follow the direction of your hand.

2. Once you have focused your dog's attention on the toy, give the *sit* command and signal. Use the toy to keep the dog interested in your hands. While the dog's attention is fixed on the toy, move the toy around, saying *"What's this?"* in an excited tone.

- *where is . . . ?*
- *what's this?*

hide-and-seek

1. You will need an assistant for the game of hide-and-seek. Play with the dog until its attention is absolutely focused on you and the toy. Ask another person to hold the dog's collar without saying a word to distract the dog from concentrating on you. Leave.

2. Allow the dog to concentrate on where you and the toy are going. A few seconds after you are out of sight, the assistant points in your direction and, using your name, says "*Where is . . . ?*" and lets the dog go. This teaches your dog to hunt for members of the family.

3. When your dog finds you, play boisterously with it. Hide-and-seek channels your dog's natural hunting instinct and can be played in the park or the woods. In a group situation, each person takes a turn hiding. Always give generous praise and encouragement when the dog finds you.

seek-back

1. One of a dog's greatest skills is its ability to detect different scents. Your dog will enjoy playing games that involve using its nose. Place your dog at your left side, wearing its leash. Holding a toy in your right hand, walk forward together. After a few paces, drop the toy.

2. Walk for about another six paces. Then encourage your dog to turn around to face the dropped toy. Offer your hand for the dog to sniff, then say "*What's this?*" as you point toward the toy. Let your dog go as soon as it recognizes the toy and heads toward it.

3. Don't hold your dog back. If it wants to run, drop the leash and follow. While it retrieves the toy, pick up the leash. Encourage the dog to give you the toy, perhaps playing a game of tug. Repeat the exercise, increasing the distance and the variety of articles.

playing to divert the dog from distractions

1• While you are out casually walking with your dog, holding the end of the leash, you may see someone coming toward you with another dog. Your own dog is concentrating on sniffing and has not noticed the other animal. So far, there is no problem.

2• Your dog sees the other dog and pulls toward it. You and your dog are now at full stretch. The more you pull the more it wants to get to the other dog. Not knowing if the other dog is friendly, you must get your dog's attention without creating a confrontation.

3• Bring your dog closer to you to get its attention, hold up a toy and say "*What's this?*" in an excited tone. When the dog comes to you, play a game of tug to distract its attention from the other dog. If necessary, turn your dog to face in a different direction.

GOLD Your dog can sit and focus its attention on a toy. It plays with the toy when you throw it. Your dog runs after you and other members of the family to play hide-and-seek. Your dog fetches an article even though it did not see the article being dropped.

4• While you are still playing, shorten the leash to get better control of your dog. Keep the game going until the distraction of the other dog and owner has passed. When you are ready to walk forward again, continue using the toy to hold your dog's attention.

SILVER Your dog can sit and focus on a toy, but jumps to grab it. Your dog runs and plays when you throw the toy. Your dog eagerly plays hide-and-seek. Your dog goes to the dropped toy but doesn't pick it up and needs you to be there to play tug.

BRONZE Your dog can sit and focus its attention on a toy, but jumps up to grab it, plays with it, and then runs away with it. Your dog eagerly plays hide-and-seek. Your dog goes to the dropped article, but sometimes picks it up and then runs away with it.

2:4 | basic training

examination and grooming

Examining and grooming your puppy on a daily basis develops its trust and confidence in you and should be regarded as an important feature of the pup's training. It also enables you to pick up early signs of possible problems before they become serious. Always seek the advice of a veterinarian before administering any treatment to your dog.

1• Use the *sit* to examine your puppy's head and chest, the *stand* to check its back, flank, and backside, and the *down* to check its underside and legs. Stroke its coat to see if it feels clean. Then stroke its fur the wrong way to expose the skin and check that it is clean.

2• Place your puppy in the *sit*, giving verbal reassurances as you handle it. Carefully touch around your pup's ears. Once your puppy is relaxed, take hold of its ear flap. Fold it back over the pup's head. Check that the ears are clean, do not smell bad, and are not hot.

3• Steady your puppy in the *sit* or *down*. Once your pup has relaxed, stroke down its leg, taking hold just above the foot. Feel and examine the pads and nails. Repeat the procedure until your puppy relaxes enough to let you examine each leg and foot.

4• Place your puppy in the *sit*. Stroke its head. Place one hand under its jaw, close to its neck. Place your other hand on top of the pup's head with your thumbs close to the upper and lower eyelid. Gently guide the lids open to expose the eye.

commands used

- *s i t*
- *d o w n*
- *s t a n d*

5. The nose and mouth areas are extremely sensitive and should always be handled carefully. The nose should be cool with no abnormal discharge, although some dogs' noses are naturally dry. The teeth should be cleaned regularly to prevent the build up of tartar and unpleasant mouth ulcers.

6. Place your puppy in the *s t a n d*. Turn and face its backside. Put your hands on either side of its body and stroke toward the tail. Grasp its tail close to the root and gently lift it. Repeat this until your pup stands still and allows you to examine the anal area.

veterinary examination

Prepare your dog for its first veterinary visit by accustoming it to grooming and home examination on a table with a non-slip surface. Your veterinarian may ask you to hold your dog and to steady it in position.

1. Steady the pup in *s i t* while its ear canal is examined. The ears should be clean, not hot and red, and should not have a strong smell. Use a cotton swab to wipe any dirt from the ear flap, but only clean as far as you can see.

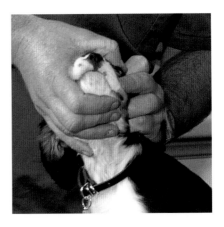

2. Most dogs do not have problems with their eyes. If tears overflow and run down your dog's face, causing a brown stain, use damp cotton to wipe it away. If the condition persists, always consult your veterinarian.

3. Hold your pup securely while its feet and nails are examined. It may need to have its nails cut before you take it out for regular exercise on hard surfaces. The veterinarian will show you the best way to do this.

4. Steady the pup in *s t a n d*. Most dogs object to having their backside touched, so it is important to train your dog to accept this type of handling during grooming sessions.

2:5

hide-and-seek

Hide-and-seek and seek-back are games in which your pup learns to use its sense of smell to find either you or a toy that you have dropped. The scent exercise develops through these games, so that in time your dog will be able to differentiate between an article with your scent and one that doesn't have your scent.

1. Hold the leash in your left hand and an article in your right hand. As you walk, drop the article to one side and behind you. If there is a breeze, help your dog by arranging the exercise so that the wind blows over the article, toward you. Continue walking forward with your dog until the article is out of sight.

2. Turn your dog around, keeping it close to you so that you can give it your scent. Hold your hand in front of your dog's nose or just under its lower jaw and allow it to sniff your hand. Don't smother your dog's nose or try to force it to take your scent. As it is sniffing, give the command *seek!*

4. When your dog finds the article, let it pick it up, then praise it and play. Ask someone to put down one or two new articles that your dog cannot physically pick up, and repeat steps 1 to 3, dropping your article among them so that your dog begins to learn to discriminate between your scent and that of others.

3. Command and signal in the direction of the article. Allow your dog to go ahead of you—don't pull it back. While the dog searches for the article, encourage it, but let it work—your dog knows more about using its nose instinctively than you can ever teach it.

handler's scent

1. Choose an article that your dog likes to pick up. Ask an assistant to put several different articles on the ground, but not too close together. Now, focus your dog's attention on its "own" article. You can achieve this by throwing the article into the scent area before you give the dog your scent and send it to find the article.

2. Next, ask your assistant to place "your" article. Take your dog to within 12 feet (3.7 m) of the scent area. Keep it by your side, facing away from the area. Have your assistant take your article using tongs or a tray so that it is not contaminated with his or her scent. Let your dog see your assistant take it.

3. Have your assistant place "your" article among the other articles. At first, let your dog see your assistant do this. As your dog becomes more experienced, use a variety of articles to keep your dog interested, hiding them among the "neutral" objects.

4. Ask your assistant to move out of the way. Then, turn your dog, keeping it by your side while you give it the scent. Allow it to sniff your hand; at the same time give the command *s e e k !* After a few seconds, send your dog to find.

5. Command *s e e k !* and signal toward the scent area, then let your dog go. While your dog is working, don't distract it. When your dog has found the article and picked it up, say *"G o o d   d o g"* and encourage it to retrieve to hand. Develop the exercise by using different articles for your dog to find, by increasing the scent area, and by using different patterns for the dropped articles.

 GOLD Your dog finds and picks up different scent articles that you drop. Your dog finds an article with your scent on it amid a variety of articles placed by an assistant. Your dog, having found an article, brings it to your hand.

 SILVER Your dog finds and picks up different scent articles that you drop. Your dog finds an article with your scent on it amid a variety of articles placed by an assistant. Your dog finds "your" article, but needs you to go to the article and play in order to retrieve it from the scent area.

 BRONZE Your dog finds a variety of articles that are dropped or hidden, but doesn't always pick them up. When "your" article is placed among others, your dog quickly loses interest in its own article and wants to play with or pick up the others. Go back to putting "your" article among articles that your dog cannot physically pick up.

2:6 basic training
retrieving

Once you have trained your pup to retrieve in the form of a game, it will be ready to develop that play into a controlled retrieving exercise. This involves first teaching your dog to tolerate having its mouth opened, and then teaching it to pick up and hold a variety of articles safely.

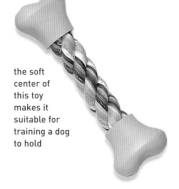

the soft center of this toy makes it suitable for training a dog to hold

1. Standing in front of your sitting dog, place your right hand under its jaw and your left hand over its muzzle. Using the fingers of your left hand, lift the dog's lips. Then, place a finger and thumb behind its canine teeth to open its mouth. Praise the dog warmly.

2. Once the dog is used to this, you can place an article, such as a toy, in its mouth. Hold the toy in your right hand. Let the dog sniff it. As you say "*Good dog!*" open the dog's mouth with your left hand. Roll the article into its mouth just behind its canine teeth. Say "*Good dog! Fetch.*"

3. Keeping your right hand under the dog's jaw, continue to hold the dog's head up. Stroking the top of its muzzle with your left hand, praise the dog and repeat the *fetch* command in a friendly tone. After a few seconds, remove the article from its mouth.

4. If your dog tries to drop the article while in the *fetch* position, make a growly "*aaAH!*" sound. When it restores its grip, in a friendly tone say "*Good dog! Fetch.*" To remove the article, use a right-hand finger to touch its tongue. As it opens its mouth, remove the article.

5. If your dog is reluctant to give up the article, don't pull; this is the trigger to grip harder. Press the dog's lips onto its teeth behind the article using the fingers of the hand placed under its jaw. When it opens its mouth to relieve the pressure, take the article.

6. If your dog has a firm grip on a small article, making it difficult to remove it by using physical manipulation, try exchanging it for a treat or a toy. Place your left hand just under its muzzle, ready to take the article when you make the exchange.

application of retrieve

1. Giving enough exercise and controlled free running to a dog could be difficult for someone unable to walk far, perhaps because of an illness or old age. Retrieving, however, is an ideal way for anyone to exercise a dog. Find a safe area where both of you will feel secure.

2. Bring a few of your dog's favorite toys. Allow your dog some freedom, then throw a toy. Encourage the dog to bring it to you. Praise the dog and throw the article again. Keep it informal and interesting by changing the article and allowing the dog some time just to play.

GOLD Your dog allows you to open its mouth. Your dog takes various articles from your hand, holds them, and allows you to take them back. Your dog holds an article, doesn't chew or drop it, and willingly puts it into your hand.

SILVER Your dog allows you to open its mouth. Your dog accepts and holds an article in its mouth only if you keep your hands in the *fetch* position and continue repeating the *fetch* command. Your dog tries to chew certain articles.

BRONZE Your dog allows you to open its mouth. Your dog takes articles into its mouth but immediately drops them. Your dog tries to run away with the article.

- *sit*
- *come!*
  Use an encouraging,
  excited tone.
- *good dog!*
- *heel*

2:7 basic training

recall

If your dog is to run free, it must learn to return instantly at your command wherever you are, whatever the distractions. This training must be carried out in as many different locations as possible. Whenever you are in a new environment, repeat this exercise. You can train the dog off the leash in a safe location.

stage 1

1. Place your dog, wearing its leash, by your left side. Give the *sit* command and signal. Step close in front of your dog, facing it. While talking to your dog, gather its leash up in your hand. Place your hands just above its muzzle and focus the dog's attention on your hands.

3. Your dog's attention was focused on your hands as it moved toward you. Stopping and lifting your hands causes the dog to sit. Praise and reward the dog. Command and signal the dog to remain sitting as you move to the *heel* position. Praising the dog completes the exercise.

2. Give the *come* command and move backward in a straight line. Keep your hands close in front of you with your dog's attention fixed on them. Continue saying "*Good dog! Come!*" After a few yards, come to a stop. Bring your feet together and simultaneously move your hands upward a couple of inches.

stage 2

1. Train your dog on a leash anywhere that is unsafe for it to be loose. With your dog in the *heel* position, take a small pace to your right. Then move forward toward the end of the leash, keeping it loose. Stop and face the dog. Give the *sit* command and signal.

2. Continue signaling your dog to sit until you are ready to call it. Or, if you think your dog might anticipate your call, repeat the *sit* command as well as signaling. Then, bring your hands into the greeting position. Wait a couple of seconds and call your dog.

3. Say the dog's name, adding "*Come!*" When your dog moves toward you, praise it, saying "*Good dog! Come!*" Begin moving backward to encourage your dog to keep moving. When it reaches you, focus its attention on your hands. Use the upward hand movement to put the dog into the *sit*.

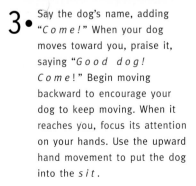

4. Praise and reward your sitting dog. Then move into the *heel* position by the side of your dog. Praising the dog again completes the exercise. In safe areas, let your dog loose to play. Then repeat Stages 1 and 2. If it is safe, do the exercise without the leash.

- *sit*
- *heel*
- *attention*

stage 3

1. With your dog on its leash, go to a safe location with few distractions. Place your dog in the *sit* at *heel* alongside your left foot. Continue repeating and signaling the *sit* command while you undo the leash. Loop the leash over your shoulder to keep your hands free.

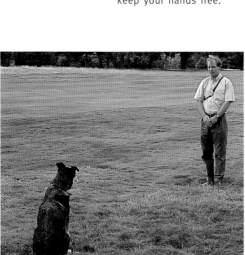

2. Ensure that there are no distractions and that it is safe to leave your dog. Still repeating and signaling the *sit* command, take a step to your right. Make sure your dog is steady. Walk forward. Check that your dog is still sitting. Give the *sit* command and signal to remind it.

3. Build on success, gradually increasing the space to ten paces. Move confidently and unhesitatingly. Stop and turn to face your dog. As you turn, be ready to remind your dog to sit using the command and signal. Then, bring your hands together in front of you and stand still.

4. After a few seconds, call your dog's name in an excited tone. Give the *attention* signal at the same time by moving your arms out to the side. As soon as your dog approaches you, bring your hands together in front of you.

5. If you keep your dog's attention focused on your hands, it will be less likely to be distracted from coming to you. It also gives the dog an incentive to move straight toward you. As your dog approaches you, encourage it by saying "*Good dog! Come!*"

6. As your dog reaches you, repeat its name, along with the *come* command. Bring your hands up slightly to place the dog in the *sit*. Praise and reward the dog. Once the dog is steadily in the *sit*, move to the *heel* position by its side.

7. While you are standing alongside your dog, continue praising and reminding it to sit. Take hold of the leash and clip it to the dog's collar. When the dog is back under control, the exercise is complete. Encourage, reassure, and praise the dog at each step of the exercise.

8. After you have praised and rewarded your dog, release it from the exercise. Take a couple of paces back. At the same time, encourage your dog to follow you. Play a game with your dog to relax its concentration after finishing the exercise.

 GOLD
In safe locations you can leave your unleashed dog in the *sit*, take ten paces, halt, turn, and wait for seven seconds before calling the dog. Your dog comes at your command and sits in front of you. Your dog stays in the *sit* until you move into the *heel* position and release it.

 SILVER
In safe locations you can leave your unleashed dog in the *sit*, walk six paces, halt, turn, and wait for five seconds before calling it. Your dog comes at your command, but needs help to sit in front of you. Your dog remains in the *sit* until you move into the *heel* position. Your dog waits while you put its leash back on.

 BRONZE
In safe locations you can leave your unleashed dog in the *sit*, walk four paces, halt, turn, and wait five seconds before calling it. Your dog is slow to come unless tempted by a treat, or runs away. Your dog needs help to sit in front of you.

- *h e e l*
  Use the appropriate
  hand signal.
- *s i t*

learning to come to heel

Coming to heel means that, from wherever your dog is, it takes the quickest, easiest route to your side without impeding your movement. This skill is used in recall, retrieve, and scent exercises, and also to move your dog from the *s i t*, in front of you, to the *h e e l* position at your side.

conventional finish to the right

1. Begin this exercise with the dog on a leash in a controlled position. Place the dog at *h e e l* on your left side, close to your leg. Hold the leash in both hands. Command and signal your dog to sit. Swivel so that you are faced reasonably close to your dog.

2. The leash will be used to guide the dog. When your dog has mastered the exercise, it will be done without a leash. Standing close in front of your dog, pass the leash to your right and then behind you. Grasp it with your left hand behind your back.

3. Repeating the *s i t* command, take a step to your left. You now have a clear path in front of you. Keep your right hand toward your dog. Use a simultaneous signal, command, and movement to guide your dog around behind you to the *h e e l* position.

4. Give the *heel* command. Use your right hand to signal to your right and at the same time walk forward. The instant your dog moves, encourage it to go behind you to your left side. Stepping aside and walking forward allows your dog free movement. Your dog should not be dragged.

5. As your dog moves behind you, bring your right hand in front of you to take hold of the leash. Now you can use your left hand to guide and encourage your dog into the *heel* position. This finish also helps teach your dog to do a right-about turn.

6. As soon as your dog arrives in the *heel* position, stop and praise it for moving correctly. Then place it in the *sit* at your side. When your dog shows confidence at moving behind you, repeat the exercise but drop the step to the side. Then, drop the forward movement as well.

- *sit*
- *heel*
- *good dog!*

continental finish to the left

1. This finish will help teach your dog to do a left turn. Place your dog on its leash in the *sit* by your left leg. Hold the leash in both hands. Swivel around so that you are faced reasonably close in front of your dog.

2. Standing in front of your dog, repeat the *sit* command. Take a step to your right. You should now have a clear path ahead of you. With your left hand, take hold of the leash close to your dog.

3. Use a simultaneous signal, command, and movement to guide your dog to turn toward you, keeping close to your left leg, as it follows: Give the *heel* command, use your left hand to signal and guide your dog toward you, as you walk forward.

5. As soon as your dog is in the correct *heel* position, in line close to your left leg, take the leash into your right hand. Stop and praise the dog while it is by your side. Once your dog knows how to turn and move with you, drop the step to the right.

4. As your dog turns to follow you forward, say "*Good dog! Heel!*" Gather up the slack of the leash in your left hand. Don't drag your dog, but use the movement to guide it into the *heel* position instead. Gradually reduce your movement and leave it entirely up to your dog.

 GOLD Your dog accomplishes both finishes on command and signal without the help of a side step or forward movement.

 SILVER Your dog can accomplish one of the finishes on command and signal without your forward movement. Your dog still needs the guidance of your forward movement to complete the other finish.

 BRONZE Your dog needs the guidance of your step to the side and forward movement to achieve both finishes.

2:9

learning to be left alone

Dogs are social animals and must be taught how to accept being alone. The more secure your pup feels, the more confident it will feel about being by itself. Puppies and dogs that are insecure require continual contact and need a safe haven. Some dogs get into trouble when left alone, and need to be confined.

1. Learning to use its cage confidently must always be a pleasant experience for your pup. Proceed gradually and with patience. Place your pup's bed in its cage. Then, set its food dish toward the back of the cage. Call your pup to you and encourage it to go into the cage to eat.

2. Leave the cage door open. Remain nearby and praise the pup so it relaxes and eats its food. Repeat the procedure until your pup freely enters the cage at different times of the day. Increase the time it spends in its cage by placing toys and treats inside for the pup to discover.

3. When your pup is happily wandering into the cage, start to close the door. Encourage your pup to play or look for food. Before it starts to get worried about being closed in, divert its attention away from the door. Then, without saying a word, open the door and quietly walk away.

4. Put something in the cage that will amuse the pup for some time, and close the door. Gradually increase the time your pup is confined on a daily basis. If it cries, go to the cage and divert its attention away from the door. Without speaking, open the door and quietly walk away.

GOLD
Your pup is happy to be left alone. When left on its own, your pup does not cause any damage. Your pup does not bark when left on its own.

SILVER
Your pup can be left alone for a short time. If left alone in a room, your pup scratches the door.

BRONZE
You cannot leave your pup by itself because it barks for attention and company.

2:10 | basic training

release from exercise

Your dog needs to know when it is on duty and when it can relax; therefore, it is important that your dog understands when an exercise is complete. After spending time concentrating on learning an exercise, your dog needs a clear signal indicating that it can relax.

dog in down or sit-stay

1. After completing the *sit, down,* and *stay* exercises, return to your dog. Stand by its side, put it back on its leash, and praise it in this position. After a few seconds, give the *OK* command as you move backward, encouraging your dog to turn on the spot and come to you.

2. Having trained your dog to remain still, it is important not to encourage it to move forward when you release it from the exercise. Turning your dog toward you when you release it helps prevent this.

dog in stand-stay

1. After completing the *stand-stay* exercise, return to your dog's side. Put it back on its leash and praise it in the *stand* without letting it move. Hold the leash close to its collar. After a couple of seconds, command *OK*.

2. Release your dog from the *stand* by turning it to the left. This prevents your dog from walking forward in anticipation of the end of the exercise.

dog in sit at heel

1. Many exercises, or parts of exercises, finish with your dog sitting by your side.

2. As you give the OK command, step backward a few paces and encourage your dog to turn toward you to play.

dog in sit in front

1. Release your dog after an exercise, or after part of an exercise, that finishes with your dog sitting in front of you. As your dog sits in front of you, praise it and focus its attention on you. After a few seconds, give the OK command and run backward to encourage your dog to play.

2. As you gain more control of your dog, you do not always have to put it back on the leash.

GOLD Your dog waits for the OK command and signal before moving at the end of all exercises.

SILVER Your dog waits for the OK command and signal before moving at the end of some exercises only.

BRONZE Your dog gets very excited, jumps around, and is difficult to bring back under control.

commands used
- *stop*
- *sit*
- *OK — away
  you go*
Use a friendly tone.

2:11 basic training

release to play

Dogs with good manners make good publicity. In addition, teaching your dog to respect your control may ultimately save its life. Your dog will learn to wait until you consider it safe to have a free run instead of jumping out of the car and charging around out of control.

1. Park your car in a safe place. Holding your dog's leash, command your dog to *stop* before opening the car door. Repeat the *stop* command again while the door is open. Keep your dog steady as you attach the leash to its collar.

3. Hold the dog's collar high on its neck to maintain close control. Grasp the leash firmly using both hands because your dog will be excited in anticipation of going for a run. Walk to a safe area with your dog under control.

5. Check again that it is safe. When you are sure, give your dog the "*OK — away you go*" command, letting go of its collar and signaling forward with your right hand.

2. Grasp the leash securely. If your dog is still waiting in the car after a few seconds, call it by its name. Keep the dog close to you on a short leash while you close the car door and prepare to leave your car.

4. Look around you to check that it will be safe for your dog to have a free run. Place your dog in the *sit* by the side of your left leg. Holding its collar with your left hand, keep your dog steady and undo its leash.

 GOLD In the car, your dog waits quietly for its leash to be put on and then waits to be called out of the car. Your dog walks under control and sits while you take off its leash. Your dog waits until you command that it can have a free run.

 SILVER In the car, your dog waits for its leash to be put on and then waits to be called out of the car. Your dog gets excited and pulls on its leash. Your dog sits as you take off its leash, but wiggles to be free to run.

 BRONZE In the car, your dog gets excited and squirms while you put on its leash. Your dog jumps out of the car before you call it. Your dog pulls on the leash. Your dog sits, but then wiggles to be free to run.

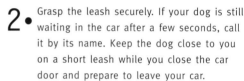

commands used

- *b e d*
  Use a friendly, positive tone.
- *g o o d   d o g !*

basic training

2:12
learning to go to bed

Because it is a pack animal, your dog will always prefer to be with you. However, this is not always convenient. It is an advantage to be able to send your dog to its bed, not as punishment, but at mealtimes, when you have visitors, or anytime you don't want your dog under your feet.

1. Encourage your dog to associate its bed with pleasure and boost its confidence at being away from you. Place your dog's bed, or some of its bedding, near your chair. Kneel by the bed, pat it, and call your dog. Praise your dog and play with it on the bed.

3. Praise the dog when it gets into the bed. If it tries to leave, pat the bed, repeating "*Good dog! Bed!*" Keep the dog there for a few seconds, praise it, and then let it move away. Use the *b e d* command and gesture every time you are going to sit in the chair.

2. Sit on the chair. Entice your dog into its bed using a toy or a treat. Pat the bedding and say "*Bed*" in a pleasant tone. Don't make your dog take up any particular position, just encourage it to settle down, saying "*Good dog!*" Observe your dog.

4. Over time and inch-by-inch, move the bed toward its permanent position. Always make being in bed a pleasant experience and not a punishment. Continue associating the *b e d* command with its bed until your dog goes to it happily even when commanded from a distance.

 GOLD Your dog goes to its bed on command and settles down. Your dog remains in its bed until you say it can come back out.

 SILVER You have to take your dog to its bed. Your dog will settle down if it has something to amuse it. You have to repeat the *b e d* command in order to make the dog stay in its bed until you are ready to let it move.

 BRONZE Your dog will settle down only if its bed is close to your chair and it has something to amuse it. You have to repeat the *b e d* command in order to make the dog stay in its bed until you are ready to release it.

advanced

To move your dog's training into this level, you should have obtained gold medals at all the previous levels. The importance of advanced training lies in both the combination of exercises and your ability to command and control your dog at a distance. In this section, you will learn how to adapt and combine exercises, creating new interest for you and your dog. Being with your dog should be fun and pleasurable for you and your family. If you want to enter your pup in competitions, join a club to find out about the rules and requirements.

training

sendaway

commands used

- *s i t*
- *d o w n*
- *l o o k*
  Use an excited tone.
- *a w a y*
  Use an encouraging tone.

In many countries the "sendaway" forms part of competition working tests. The dog should go unhesitatingly to a designated area where it is stopped in either the ***s t a n d***, ***s i t***, or ***d o w n***. The dog may then be sent to the left or right to a second point; or, it may be recalled to the handler; or, the handler may go to the dog before completing the exercise.

1. To train your dog to go away happily requires an incentive. Also, in order for your dog to go in a straight line, it needs to focus on something at a distance. To achieve this, you need an object, such as a piece of mat, that is different from its usual toys.

2. First, you need to teach your dog only to play with the mat when you are holding it; when the mat is on the ground, it acts as a focus for your dog to go to. When your dog reaches the mat, control it into the *s i t* or *d o w n*, so that it does not wander around.

3. When you are playing, say "*L o o k*" in an excited tone, so that the dog associates this activity with the mat. As the exercise develops, the *l o o k* command will encourage your dog to look straight and focus on a distant object. Now, hold your dog at your side and throw the mat a short distance ahead.

4. As the mat falls, say "*L o o k*." Give a hand signal toward the mat and the *a w a y* command as you let the dog go. When your dog reaches the mat, immediately praise it and control it into the *d o w n*. Wait a few seconds, release your dog, pick up the mat, and play.

commands used

- *h e e l*
- *s i t*
- *l o o k*
- *d o w n*
- *a w a y*

6. Say "*L o o k*" to focus your dog's attention on the mat. Simultaneously give a hand signal toward the mat and the *a w a y* command. Follow your dog so you can praise it. Put your dog in the *d o w n*, then release it and play.

5. The next stage is to increase the distance between you and the mat. Place your dog in the *h e e l* position and give the *s i t* command. Walk away about ten paces and place the mat on the ground. Move three paces toward your dog and a little to the side.

7. Over time move closer to your dog until you can send it away while you are standing by its side. Your dog will gradually learn to focus on the mat when you say "*L o o k*," will happily go straight to the mat at your hand signal and *a w a y* command, and will go into position on command and remain still until you go over and praise it. ·

8. Next, have an assistant place the mat about 30 yards (27.5 m) in front of you and your dog. When the assistant is out of sight, continue the exercise as before. Now turn the dog away so that it does not see the mat being placed. When the assistant is out of sight, turn the dog toward the mat and position it in the *s i t* by your side.

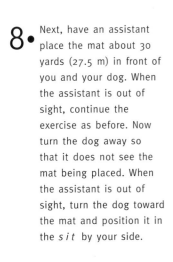

9. Give the *l o o k* command. As soon as your dog is looking straight toward the mat, send it and continue the exercise as before. Repeat, making the sendaway point fun to go to.

sendaway to markers

2. Say "*Look*" as soon as your dog looks straight at the marker and mat. Give the hand signal and *away* command. When your dog reaches the sendaway area, control it into position, then go to it to praise and release it. Keeping the marker and mat in position, repeat the exercise, taking the dog further away from the marker each time.

1. Once your dog has mastered the first stage, you need to transfer its attention from the mat to other distant markers. Ask your assistant to place a marker, such as a small white flag, then put the mat in front of it. Do not let your dog see this. Place your dog by your side facing toward the marker and mat.

3. Build your dog's experience by reducing the size of the marker, and alternate between using and not using the mat. Whenever you use a new marker, start by using the mat, too. Always use the *look* command to get your dog to look straight before sending it away. Command it into position and wait a few moments before going to praise it.

domestic use

The sendaway exercise is mainly used in competitions. However, training your dog to go away from you can be useful when sending your dog to bed or in situations where it would be safer to have your dog ahead of you, such as walking down stairs or along a narrow path.

 GOLD Your dog plays with the mat, but understands that when it is on the ground, it must stay still on it. Your dog looks in the direction of the sendaway when you say "*Look!*" and goes away when commanded. You can control your dog at a distance. You can send your dog 30 yards (27.5 m) away to its mat.

 SILVER Your dog plays with the mat and stays still on it when it is on the ground. You can leave your dog and stand halfway between it and the mat. Your dog looks toward the mat when you give the *look* command. You need to follow your dog to the mat to control it.

 BRONZE Your dog plays with the mat when you are holding it, but then picks it up off the ground. You can leave your dog in the *sit* while you place the mat. You have to stay close to the mat to control your dog.

advanced training | # 3:2
heelwork

Heelwork, unlike other exercises, does not have a set beginning, middle, and end. There is no set pattern to train toward; the content depends on the trainer. Stop within your dog's concentration span while it is still eager and maintaining full attention and reasonable accuracy. Your dog's shoulder should be even with your left hip and reasonably close to you, without impeding your movement.

bringing your dog to heel from an angle

1. Heelwork involves teaching your dog how to take up the position at your side, even with your left hip. Do this as a separate exercise from the main exercise of walking to heel. Put your dog on a leash and position it at *heel*. Command and signal your pup to sit.

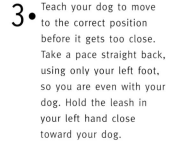

2. Take one pace to the right and one forward, keeping your left hand on the leash to steady the dog, which is now sitting behind you at an angle to your left. If you commanded your dog to heel, it would probably come in at an angle and would need to be handled into the correct position.

3. Teach your dog to move to the correct position before it gets too close. Take a pace straight back, using only your left foot, so you are even with your dog. Hold the leash in your left hand close toward your dog.

4. Give the *heel* command and simultaneously bring the leash toward your leg to signal the dog to move. As soon as the dog starts to move, encourage it to come close to your left leg. The hand signal will train the dog to move to the *heel* position when working off the leash.

5. When your dog is close to your leg, praise it and bring your left leg forward to your right, straightening the dog into the correct position. Praise your dog, then put it into the *sit* by your left leg. Always praise the dog for making the correct movement before putting it into the *sit*.

on the spot turning to the right

1. You and your dog must hold a perfect *heel* position in order to change direction together. How you turn and what signals you give will influence the standard of the turn. Put your dog in the *heel*. Exaggerate your upper body movement turning to the right. Say the pup's name and say "*Heel.*"

2. As your upper body turns, start to turn your feet. Keep your left foot close to your right and twist on the balls of your feet to help complete the turn on the spot. Keep the weight equal on both feet. Hold the leash in your left hand close to your hip.

3. As your dog learns to follow your movement and stays close, praise it, saying "*Good dog! Heel!*" As soon as your dog has learned how to follow your body signal and command, and you can turn smoothly together, eliminate the exaggerated body movement.

4. As soon as you have turned and you are balanced, step forward and praise your dog, saying "*Good dog! Heel!*" Repeat the exercise. Once you and your dog are confident, walk forward at a slow pace and perform the turn while moving. Repeat this until you gradually reach normal walking speed.

on the spot turning to the left

1. Place your dog sitting at *heel*. Turn your upper body to the left and move your left hand down the leash, close to your dog. These form the physical signals that indicate you want to turn. Simultaneously, say your dog's name and give the *heel* command.

2. Grasp the leash in front of your left leg, holding your dog close. This will help turn your dog to the left. Keeping your left foot still, place your right foot close to your left and then start to turn toward your dog.

3. Twist on the balls of your feet on the spot to initiate the turn to the left, still holding the leash with your left hand close to your leg. When you are facing to the left and have regained your balance, take a pace forward.

4. Praise your dog while it is in the *heel* position. Repeat the maneuver. This will train your dog to stay at *heel* by turning the instant you give the hand signal on the leash. Introduce the controlled left turn while moving at a slow pace and gradually increase to your normal pace.

heel

figure eight around markers

1. Figure eights teach your dog to how to hold the *heel* position by changing its pace, and how to keep close to you when going around obstacles. Place two markers approximately 15 feet (4.5 m) apart. Put your dog on its leash and start the heelwork between the markers.

2. Give the *heel* command and walk forward toward the first marker at a normal walking speed. Leave space around the marker. Use your left hand on the leash to prepare your dog to slow down its pace, while you maintain your normal pace. Circle left, praise the dog, and give the *heel* command.

3. When you have completed the turn, walk from the first marker to the second one at a normal pace. Use a slow pace when walking around the left marker and a fast pace when walking around the right marker. Help your dog maintain the *heel* position by exaggerating the paces.

4. One or two paces before you reach the second marker, encourage your dog to speed up as you circle around the marker to the right. Help the dog along, but don't drag it. Keep your dog's attention. Gradually bring the markers closer together until they are about 9 feet (2.75 m) apart.

slow and fast paces from the halt

1. Heelwork teaches your dog to pick up subtle signals that enable it to maintain the *heel* position. Move forward slowly from the *halt* position, say your dog's name, and give the *heel* command in a calm voice. To stay balanced, keep your weight slightly back as you stride forward.

2. To move from the *halt* position at a fast pace, say your dog's name in an excited tone of voice and give the *heel* command. To stay balanced, move your weight forward as you take the first stride.

changing your pace while moving

1. Changing your pace while moving is easier than from the *halt* position because it can be done gradually. Walk your dog forward at a normal pace. To prepare it to go into a slow pace, hold the leash with your left hand and slowly give the *heel* command, using a calm tone of voice. Gradually slow your pace, keeping a smooth even stride.

2. Walk forward at a normal speed. Use an excited tone of voice to get your dog's attention and to prepare it to increase the speed. Gradually lengthen your stride, leaning forward slightly as you speed up to a trot. If your dog starts to jump, don't scold it. Simply return to a normal walking speed.

handling for the breed ring

Your mannerisms and commands can also be used to teach your dog how to behave in the ring. For the show ring, however, a dog is taught to move slightly away from the handler. This way its movements are not impeded by the position or handling of the person showing the dog.

handling for the trial ring

Obedience competitions measure the maintenance and harmony of movement between the dog and the handler, which result from subtle body signals and very consistent handling. In all types of competition it is important to foster your dog's willingness by encouraging it.

GOLD

Your dog quickly reacts to your signals for the left and right on-the-spot turns. Your dog comes to *h e e l* from an angle and takes up the correct position. You can walk at normal pace around markers and your dog changes pace to stay in the *h e e l* position. Your dog stays close when you change pace in heelwork.

SILVER

Your dog can make a right on-the-spot turn but needs help on the left. Your dog correctly comes to the *h e e l* position from an angle. In the figure-eight exercise, your dog needs help making a right turn around a marker. Your dog can only manage gradual changes of pace.

BRONZE

Your dog can make an on-the-spot turn to the right but needs help turning left on the spot. You have to help your dog to come to *h e e l* from an angle. In the figure-eight exercise, your dog holds the *h e e l* position if you change your pace to assist it. Your dog can only manage gradual changes of pace.

commands used

• *h e e l*
Use a firm,
encouraging tone.

advanced training

3:3

recall to heel

Recalling a dog to the *h e e l* position is a very practical exercise.
Calling your dog to you while you are moving away from it will give your
dog more of an incentive to come to you than simply standing still and
calling it. At first, train your dog while it is wearing its leash. Leave the
dog, then call it, signaling it to *h e e l* while moving away from it.

1• Always check that it is safe for your dog
to go off and explore, although you
cannot always guarantee that things will
stay that way. Whenever you allow your
dog off the leash, have your training
incentives with you. Always expect the
unexpected in a free-run situation. If you
see that your dog is showing an interest
in going off and investigating something,
you need to win back its attention.

2• Attract your dog's
attention, then move
quickly away from the
distraction. Use the *h e e l*
command and signal and
have a toy or treat in
your hand. Moving away
from your dog reduces its
confidence and it will be
more inclined to follow
you than go into an
unknown situation.

3• When your dog reaches
you, keep moving; make
it exciting for your dog to
stay close to you. Control
your dog by keeping its
attention. Reward and
praise your dog; put it
back on its leash until it
is safe to let your dog
free again.

 GOLD Your dog responds and moves to the *h e e l*
position from a free-run situation and stays
with you. Your dog allows you to put on its
leash and lets you walk it away from
distractions.

 SILVER Your dog needs an added incentive to walk
away from a distraction. If you have a toy or
treat, your dog will move to the *h e e l*
position. You need to hold your dog by the
collar to keep it under control.

 BRONZE Your dog sits and waits to be called to the
h e e l position when on its leash. Off the
leash your dog is easily distracted by other
dogs or people and you have to run away
before your dog comes after you. You have
to put your dog on the leash to control it
when there are distractions.

● *sit*
Use a positive tone.

3:4

positions

Your dog must learn to understand the *sit*, *down*, and *stand* positions, and must know how to take them up on command and/or signal before you leave it. You will need to have confidence in each other. Slowly build up the exercise, gradually increasing the time and distance. Always return to your dog to praise it; do not return to your dog to correct it.

stages of training

Training with other dogs teaches your dog how to concentrate in the midst of distractions and builds its confidence. Always return to praise your dog in position at the end of each stage. (Owners and dogs are numbered from left to right.)

1 • The dogs are positioned in the *sit* (one off its leash).
2 • The handler moves a short distance away from the leashed dog, giving the *sit* signal.
3 • The dog is off the leash. The handler is at a short distance, ready with the *sit* hand signal if necessary.
4 • The dogs are off the leash. The handler is standing relaxed and away from the dogs.

sit-stay

1• There will be occasions when it is necessary to tie up your dog and leave it for a short time. Select somewhere safe where there is little to disturb your dog. Use a fixed collar that fits well and make sure the leash is secure.

2• Put your dog into the *sit*, close to where you are going to leave it, for example, by a post. Securely tie the leash to the post above your dog's head height so your dog cannot get entangled in it. Don't tie your dog close to barriers that it might be able jump over.

3• Turn your dog to face the direction you are going. Put it into the *sit* and reassure it. Confidently walk away. Just before going out of sight, glance back to check that your dog is all right; then go completely out of sight. Repeat the exercise, gradually increasing the time you are out of sight.

4• Return, but keep quiet until you are close to your dog. Praise it in position, saying "*Good dog! Sit!*" Untie it and continue your walk. This not only trains your dog to remain in position when you go out of sight, but to keep still until you return and say it can move.

- *down*
Use a low, positive tone of voice.
- *heel*
- *good dog!*

training down out of sight

1. Choose an area with few distractions, fairly close to where you intend to go out of sight. Give the *down* command and signal. Bend down to take the leash off the dog and quietly praise it. Stand up and repeat the *down* command and signal.

2. After a few seconds, take a small pace to your right to check that your dog is steady; then continue to walk out of sight. Choose a destination where you can see your dog but your dog cannot see you, such as behind a hedge or bush. Completely go out of the dog's sight.

3. Gradually increase the time that you are out of sight, but always return to your dog before it thinks about moving. Stay out of sight until you return to your dog. Don't let it see you if you check on it.

4. When you return to your dog, don't make it nervous by staring at it. Confidently walk to the *heel* position. Watch your dog for any indication that it may break position, such as drawing its legs under itself to get up. Be ready to give the *down* hand signal and to reassure it.

GOLD
Your dog can stay in the *sit* for two minutes, the *down* for four minutes, and the *stand* for one minute, in sight of you, off its leash. Your dog waits while you return and put the leash back on it, praise it, and finish the exercise. You can leave your dog out of sight in the *sit* for one and a half minutes and the *down* for four minutes, then return and finish the exercise.

SILVER
Your dog can stay in the *sit* for one minute, the *down* for three minutes, and the *stand* for half a minute, in sight of you, off its leash. Your dog waits while you return and put the leash back on it, praise it, and finish the exercise. You can leave your dog out of sight in the *sit* for one minute and the *down* for two minutes, then return and finish the exercise.

5. Don't say anything unless you see that your dog is about to move. If this happens, recommand and reassure it in position. After a couple of seconds, bend down and praise your dog in the *down*, saying "*Good dog! Down!*" Put it back on its leash; then release it from position.

BRONZE
Your dog can stay in the *sit* for one minute and the *down* for two minutes on its leash. Your dog holds the *stand* position for 30 seconds on the leash while you are standing by its side. Your dog stays in the *down* while you go out of sight for one minute only if it is tied up.

90

commands used

- *sit*
- *stand*
  Use a firm but
  encouraging tone.
- *good dog!*

advanced training

3:5
examination

It is important to build up your dog's confidence so that it will accept being handled by strangers. Whether it is being handled for the show ring, the obedience ring, grooming, or for veterinary examinations, your dog inevitably will encounter situations where it is handled. For practical reasons, the dog must learn to remain still in each of the positions.

1. Ask an assistant to help you introduce the formal examination to your dog. Begin in a relaxed manner with your dog on its leash in the *sit*. Your helper should approach from the side and talk to you, allowing the dog to sniff him or her. Meanwhile, you reassure the dog calmly, saying "*Good dog. Sit.*" The command is repeated to reassure the dog in position.

2. Next, your helper should approach from the front, talking to you and not to the dog. If your dog responds to treats, ask your helper to hold some. When your dog leans forward to sniff, your helper can reward it. Say "*Sit*" to steady your dog and when it takes the treat, say "*Good dog.*" Once your dog has learned to accept someone coming close to it while it is in the *sit*, repeat the exercise while your dog is in the *stand*.

3. To start an examination, ask your assistant to approach from the side and to talk quietly to you and the dog. Ask your assistant to pet the dog's back. As the dog is being petted, give the *stand* command and praise the dog. Gradually increase the amount that your assistant touches your dog.

4. Do not let your dog become stressed or start to move away. Continue this exercise until your dog tolerates being fully examined by your friends. Always be ready to help keep your dog standing still. Do not allow strangers to touch your dog until it is totally relaxed.

- *stand*
- *sit*

dog being examined on a table

If your dog is to be examined on a table, pick it up and place it there, allowing it to relax before putting it in the *stand*. Keep the dog steady while the judge examines its head, ears, mouth, and teeth. You can talk to your dog to make it feel confident and reassured.

judge examining the rear legs

Judges have different methods of examining a dog. Some may stand over your dog, which may make it feel insecure. Others may bend down to the dog's level while they are checking the muscle tone. A variety of methods add to your dog's experience.

judge approaching from the front

Once you have trained your dog to accept being fully examined by a wide variety of friends and strangers, it is ready to experience a show. In this new environment, always be confident and ready to help and reassure your dog. Here, the dog is standing still while the judge approaches.

assessment of the dog's overall conformation

Your dog is the one being examined, but you, too, must stay cool and not get agitated. The aim is to make your dog look its best, but don't forget to praise it and ensure that it is happy. Remember, you will always be taking the best dog home.

GOLD

Your dog takes up the *stand* and remains still while you, a friend, or a family member examine it. Your dog takes up the *stand* and allows your veterinarian to examine it. Your dog takes up the *stand* and allows a stranger to examine it fully.

SILVER

Your dog takes up the *stand* and remains still when you and/or a family member examines it. Your dog takes up the *stand* for a friend to examine it fully. Your dog takes up the *sit* and allows a stranger to approach and praise it. You have to help your dog to stay still while your veterinarian examines it.

BRONZE

Your dog takes up the *stand* and remains still when you examine it. You have to help your dog to stand still for you or a family member to examine it. Your dog sits still when a friend approaches and praises it. Your dog won't stay still when a stranger approaches or when your veterinarian tries to examine it.

commands used

- *s p e a k !*
  Use an excited tone.
- *q u i e t*
  Use a calm tone.
- *g o o d   d o g !*

advanced training

3:6

learning to bark on command

Teaching your dog to bark on command can be useful for personal defense or as home security. Use a subtle signal to stimulate your dog to bark—one that an intruder won't recognize or one that will make a stranger think twice. Training a dog to bark on command also enables you to teach it to be quiet on command.

1. Ask someone to approach in a menacing way. A gated area is ideal because your dog can see, but not harm, your assistant. As soon as your dog barks, say "*S p e a k !*" in an excited tone. Encourage and reward it. Immediately re-stimulate your dog to bark two or three times in quick succession.

2. Repeat this until your dog barks on your first command and continues until you lower your hand to reward it. Repeat the exercise without the assistant. Say "*S p e a k !*" and give your hand signal. The instant your dog barks, encourage it to continue, then reward it. Repeat until your dog reacts to the command and signal.

3. Next, take your dog to an area that is completely away from the stimulus of the gate or other things that could make it bark. Say its name and focus its attention on your hand signal. Give the *s p e a k* command in a very excited tone. As soon as your dog barks, encourage it to continue saying "*G o o d d o g ! S p e a k !*" Lower your hand and reward it.

4. Now teach your dog to stop barking on command. Make your dog bark by giving the *s p e a k* command and encourage it to continue with the raised hand signal. Lower your hand. Your dog now associates this with a treat and will stop barking to take the food reward. When your dog stops barking, wait a couple of seconds, softly saying "*Q u i e t*," and then reward it for not barking.

GOLD Your dog barks on your command and signal without any other stimulus. Your dog stops barking on command.

SILVER Your dog barks on your command and signal only when it has some form of stimulus, such as someone coming to the door. Your dog stops barking when given a reward.

BRONZE Your dog only barks if stimulated by something; it does not respond to the command and signal alone. Your dog only stops barking when it is taken away from the stimulus and rewarded with a treat.

3:7 | advanced training

scenting strangers

Because of its ability to detect and discriminate minute odor molecules,
your dog "views" the world through its nose. It is impossible for us to
appreciate this ability. It has been described as being able to look at a
pizza "with the works" and being able to identify each individual
ingredient at a glance.

stage 1

1. Introduce this exercise as a game of seek-back. Choose an open area with as few distractions as possible. Ask a friend to bring two similar articles, such as an old pair of gloves, for your dog to find. Let your dog off its leash and walk with the wind on your backs.

2. Ask your friend to drop a glove when your dog is not looking. For the first training session, choose an area of clean ground with short grass to give your dog the opportunity to see the dropped glove. After the glove has been dropped, continue walking for a few yards.

3. Call your dog. Hold it by the collar, but it doesn't have to sit. Ask your friend to let your dog sniff the other glove. At the same time say "*S e e k !*" This command is the trigger for the dog to search for and match the last scent given.

4● Hold your dog and take the glove from your friend. As your dog sniffs it say "*S e e k !*" Face toward the dropped glove and allow the dog to either see or smell it. As soon as it shows any inclination toward the dropped glove, signal and command "*S e e k !*" and let your dog go.

5● Allow your dog to travel some distance before following behind it. Keep quiet while your dog is searching. The scent may have drifted through the air some distance from the glove, but letting your dog work this out by itself will give it confidence.

6● When your dog finds the glove and picks it up, encourage it to retrieve it to hand. If the dog is slow to pick it up, don't nag. Go to your dog and have a game. Your dog has, in fact, completed the scent exercise but needs to be stimulated to retrieve.

7● When your dog retrieves the glove make a big fuss and play a game. Don't keep repeating the exercise because it should be fun. Develop your dog's scent skills by having a variety of pairs of articles, including cloth, and by choosing the type of ground where the article will be hidden.

- *sit*
- *seek!*

1. You need the help of two assistants to develop this scent exercise. One provides and places three or four articles to make up a scent pattern. The other provides and scents two articles of cloth. One is placed in the scent pattern while you keep your dog facing away.

2. When the cloth has been placed in the scent area, turn your dog around and place it in the *sit*. Take the second cloth, with the assistant's scent on it. Hold it by the corners so as not to contaminate it with your scent— your dog must be able to retrieve the matching cloth.

3. Allow your dog to sniff the cloth. While your dog is sniffing, say *"Seek!"* The more confident and experienced a dog becomes, the less time it needs to absorb a scent— but never force your dog to take a scent.

4. When your dog has the scent, stand up and say *"Seek!"* Let your dog get to work; keep quiet. Just let your dog pick up the cloth and return it to hand. If your dog is slow to return with the cloth, encourage it by running away instead of repeatedly commanding it.

 GOLD Your dog finds and picks up an article dropped by a friend. Your dog retrieves a cloth. Your dog finds a stranger's scent on a piece of cloth among three different articles.

 SILVER Your dog finds and picks up an article dropped by a friend. Your dog picks up a piece of cloth but tries to run away with it. Your dog goes to the scent area and finds the correct cloth, but you need to be close to prevent it from running away with the cloth and playing with it.

 BRONZE Your dog finds an article dropped by a friend but runs away and plays with it. Your dog finds a cloth but chews it and plays with it. Your dog finds a cloth with a stranger's scent on it, but wants to play with the other articles. Retrain your dog how to retrieve and place articles that it cannot pick up in the scent pattern.

advanced training

3:8
retrieve

This formal retrieve exercise consists of four commands. The *sit* command steadies the dog in the *heel* position while you throw an article. The *fetch* command, said while the dog goes toward the article, instructs the dog to pick up the article and hold it. The *come* command tells the dog to return and sit in front of you, holding the article until you take it. The *heel* command tells the dog to go to heel and sit by your side.

1. Choose articles that your dog has been trained to hold and pick up. You should use a dumbell if you are considering trials or obedience competitions. Take your dog off its leash and put it in the *sit* at *heel*. Hold the retrieve article in your right hand. Give the *sit* command and signal to your dog.

2. Throw the article. If your dog is eager, it may run after the article as soon as you throw it. Practice commanding your dog to sit and pretend to throw. Or, holding its collar with your left hand as you throw, alternate between going to get the article yourself and sending your dog.

3. After a few seconds, give the *fetch* command and signal. When your dog has left you, bring your hands together into the greeting position in front of you. Stand still. You need to keep your dog enthusiastic. If your dog is slow, don't nag it. Simply turn the exercise into play.

4. Don't stare at your dog while it is returning with the article. This can make your dog nervous and cause it to slow down. If your dog returns slowly, turn and run, encouraging your dog to chase you. When it reaches you, turn to it and play. Then take the article.

- *sit*
- *fetch*
- *heel*

5• Encourage your dog to sit close in front of you with its head up. As it sits, anticipate any mouthing or possible dropping of the article. Never shout, but be ready to help keep the article in its mouth, placing one hand under its jaw while your other hand strokes the top of its muzzle.

6• Quietly praise the dog. Then use both hands to take the article. Don't lunge. If you think your dog is going to drop the article as you move your hands, repeat the previous step and then take it. Train your dog to hold the article while you move your hands around its muzzle.

7• To stop your dog from anticipating going to heel, don't do the finish every time. Command your dog to *sit* while you move to the *heel* position yourself. After a couple of seconds, release your dog.

8• Sometimes you should do the finish when your dog is steady. Give the *heel* command and signal to your dog. When you practice the retrieve, use a variety of articles to maintain your dog's interest. Vary the distance that you throw the article. Every time you introduce a new article, give your dog the chance to experience holding it in its mouth before doing the retrieve.

9• When your dog is in the *sit* at *heel*, praise it and then release it. Play a game together before repeating the exercise. In any exercise, if your dog fails at any stage, isolate that individual part of the exercise and practice it. Do not keep repeating the entire exercise.

directional retrieve

1. Your dog must be able to perform the formal retrieve. Choose two articles that your dog is eager to retrieve. This gives the dog an incentive to take your direction. Have your dog off its leash sitting at *heel*. Give the *sit* command, walk six paces forward, halt, and turn to face your dog.

2. Don't throw the article too far to begin with. Throw one article to the right and one to the left. As you throw, give the *sit* command to keep your dog steady. Often, dogs will go to the last object thrown, so keep your dog's attention focused on you.

3. Give a very clear physical gesture to your right and give the *fetch* command to instruct your dog to retrieve the article. Concentrate on the directional signal and the command. Don't use the words "right" or "left"; this gets confusing and will vary depending on whether your dog is facing you or going away from you.

4. In case your dog decides to investigate the other article, ensure a successful retrieve by moving toward the intended article. As the exercise develops, use different articles and increase the distances. This teaches your dog to take directions and can be applied to other exercises involving searching.

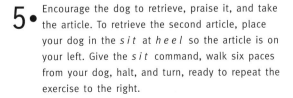

5. Encourage the dog to retrieve, praise it, and take the article. To retrieve the second article, place your dog in the *sit* at *heel* so the article is on your left. Give the *sit* command, walk six paces from your dog, halt, and turn, ready to repeat the exercise to the right.

GOLD
Your dog is steady in the *sit* at *heel* when you throw an article. Your dog goes to the article, retrieves it on command, and returns to the present position. Your dog allows you to take the article and is steady until you complete the exercise. Your dog takes your directional signals to retrieve an article.

SILVER
Your dog holds the *sit* until you command it to retrieve. Your dog needs help to return to the present position and to hold the article. You have to stay close to your dog when directing it to retrieve.

BRONZE
You have to hold your dog as you throw the article, you have to help it to return, and then help it to hold the article. On the directional retrieve, your dog anticipates and doesn't wait to be directed. Your dog runs to the first article, retrieves it, and then drops it to go to the second article.

commands used

- *sit* or *down*, depending on the position you want your pup to hold when it stops. Use a firm tone.
- *good dog!*

stop or drop on command at a distance

The ability to control your dog at a distance could save its life because it means you are able to stop your dog in an emergency. Sometimes it may be safer to stop your dog away from you than to call it to you. In some countries, this exercise must be performed in obedience trials.

1. While you are out walking your dog, or letting it enjoy a free run, you may unexpectedly hear or see some potential danger. There may not be time for your dog to get to you or for you to get to your dog, yet you must control your dog to keep it out of danger.

2. A whistle is very useful for attracting your dog's attention at a distance. Blow the whistle and give your dog the *sit* command and signal. Use a clear hand signal and take a step toward your dog. Your dog's attention will be focused on the hand signal. Repeat the *sit* command.

3. Even after the potential danger has passed, do not allow your dog to anticipate coming to you, ever. Go to your dog. Continue to use the hand signal and the *sit* command while you are walking toward it to make sure it remains still.

4. The instant you get to your dog, the most important thing is to make sure it is under control. Put it back on its leash; while you are attaching its leash, make a fuss and praise the dog, saying *"Good dog!"*

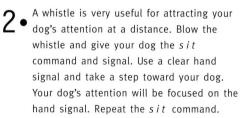

5. Once the dog is on its leash, make a great deal of fuss over it and walk away from the danger. In a real emergency, you will fully appreciate the effort you put into training your dog.

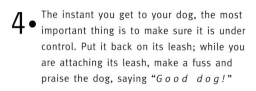

commands used
- *h e e l*
- *s i t*
- *d o w n*

training the stop

1. To train your dog to stop on command, go to an area that has few distractions. Place your dog at *h e e l* and give the *s i t* command and signal. Leave it and walk ten paces away (this will be increased over time), halt, turn, and face your dog.

3. To get an instant response, move toward your dog and give the *s i t* or *d o w n* command and signal. Repeat the exercise, reducing your movement toward your dog. Always be ready to move toward it, however, to achieve an instant stop.

2. If your dog moves in anticipation of being called, be ready to give the *s i t* command and signal. Wait a few seconds and enthusiastically call your dog. When your dog is approximately half way to you, bring your hand up in a signal and step forward to stop it.

4. During training, always go to your dog and praise it for stopping and taking up position. Occasionally finish the exercise there. Other times, recommand it into the *s i t* or the *d o w n* and leave it. Take ten paces or so and turn; wait a few seconds. Then call it to you and make a big fuss.

GOLD You can leave your dog and walk away 15 paces. You can call your dog and stop it at any distance, where it will go into the commanded position. You can go up to your dog, praise it, leave it again, and call it to hand.

SILVER You can leave your dog and walk away 15 paces. You can call your dog and stop it in position if you go toward it. You have to repeat the command and signal. After you have praised it, you can leave your dog and it comes happily to hand on command.

BRONZE You can leave your dog and walk away ten paces. You can command your dog into the *s i t* or *d o w n* only if you move toward it. You cannot stop your dog once you have called it, and it comes close to you before it takes up position.

3:10

jumping

Dogs have fun jumping and it provides them with good exercise. Jumping also teaches a dog how to negotiate obstacles. Dogs naturally jump around and over things while they are playing, but formal jump training should not start until the pup is physically mature. This will vary according to the breed and size, so check with your veterinarian.

clear jump

1. Start with the clear jump set at its lowest point. Put your dog on a fixed collar and leash. Before starting, familiarize your dog with the jump, letting it have a sniff and a walk around it. Hold your dog's leash in your left hand, but leave enough slack so that you can easily allow it to go loose.

2. Stand about six paces away from the jump. Walk your dog to the jump and step over it with your dog. Praise your dog as it lands. The next time you approach the jump, watch your dog. When it takes off, give the *over* command. Step over the jump with the dog and praise it.

3. Repeat step 2 until your dog can do it off its leash. Next, leave your dog about 5 feet (1.5 m) away from the jump and stand close to the other side of the jump. Call your dog and as it moves toward you, give the *over* command and signal. Praise your dog as it lands.

4. Continue calling your dog to you over the jump. Then stand to the side and signal it to jump. Gradually increase the height of the jump. Once your dog happily jumps on your command, start to control your dog when it lands, commanding it to take up a position. Then go to it and praise it.

long jump

1. Start with your dog on its leash. Place two or three barriers close together. Go with your dog, giving the *over* as it approaches each barrier and praising it on landing. Repeat this without the leash; then leave your dog in the *sit* about 5 feet (1.5 m) away. Stand by the first barrier and command and signal your dog to jump.

2. When your dog jumps with confidence, start to control it when it lands by commanding it into position. Go to it and praise it. Don't overexert your dog or increase the height or length of the jumps too quickly. Gradually develop your dog's physical and mental abilities.

jumping into cars

1. Make sure that the area inside the car where you want your dog to jump is clear. Take your dog close to the car so it can look inside. Pat the area inside the car to focus your dog's attention on the spot where you want it to jump.

2. Encourage your dog to jump as you signal and command it into your car. Some older dogs may need to take a running start. Praise the dog the instant it gets completely into the car.

GOLD You can leave your dog in the *sit* while you stand by the side of the clear jump and the long jump. On your command and signal, your dog jumps and remains still and waits for you to go to it and praise it.

SILVER You can leave your dog in the *sit* while you stand by the clear jump and the long jump. On your command and signal, your dog jumps. When it lands, your dog needs you to go to it to control it.

BRONZE You have to keep your dog on its leash at all times to control it to jump and to keep it still when it lands.

problem

Most problems are the manifestation of one or more underlying causes, such as boredom, insufficient physical and mental exercise, lack of constructive training, or failure to socialize for everyday occurrences. Many problems can be controlled and some can be stopped. Unless the cause is addressed, however, the problem will likely reoccur. The solution may include modifying your own behavior.

Unwanted home-based behavior often occurs when you aren't there to witness it. It is important that when you do become aware of a problem, your response doesn't create a greater problem. Menacing behavior on your part may cause your dog to go into defense mode, to run away, or in the worst case, to become aggressive.

solving

● *n o !*
Use a firm but not
an aggressive tone.

4:1 | **problem** solving

keeping the pup off the furniture

Prevention is better than a cure. When you leave a room, take your pup
with you. Teach it that it has its own bed. When you see that your pup is
about to go onto furniture say *"N o !"* and then praise it for not doing so.

1• You cannot teach your pup to stay off the furniture if you aren't there. When you are out, your pup is free to wander where it wants, and it may jump onto a comfortable chair, curl up, and go to sleep.

2• If you open the door and see your pup on the chair, quietly and calmly approach without giving it any cause for concern. Get very close to your pup and take hold of its collar. If it is surprised, reassure it.

3• You can only control your pup if you are consistent and clear in your intentions. The action of getting off the chair and the accompanying hand signal to the floor must be simultaneous. Hold the collar and use it to assist your pup off the furniture. Use your other hand to give the signal.

4. While your pup is getting off the furniture, give the *off* command so that it associates the command with going to the floor. When it is on the floor, warmly praise it. Repeat this procedure every time you find your pup on the furniture.

5. Your pup will begin to anticipate your approach and start to move off the furniture by itself. At this stage, you can give the *off* command and signal from a distance. Remember to praise your pup, however, when it reaches the floor.

what not to do

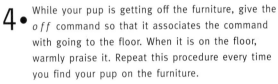

When you open the door and see your pup on the furniture, never threaten it with shouting or aggressive physical gestures. Your pup will react by defending itself or by running away looking ashamed. This behavior doesn't mean that your pup knows it has done something wrong; it only shows that it is frightened of your approach.

● see: feedback, p. 38 and learning to go to bed, p. 75

 GOLD Your pup no longer goes onto the furniture and has learned to go into its bed. Your pup responds if you say "*No!*" when you see it approaching the furniture.

 SILVER Your pup responds when you say "*No!*" if you see it approaching the furniture. Your pup has learned to go to its bed. When left alone your pup gets onto the furniture.

 BRONZE You have to say "*No!*" repeatedly before your pup obeys. If you aren't keeping an eye on your pup, it will go on the furniture. Your pup is still learning to go to its bed.

4:2 problem solving

excessive barking

Dogs vary their bark according to what they want to convey. A dog's bark can be used as a rallying cry, asking the rest of the pack to come and back it up. Or it can be used to express surprise at the sight or sound of something that it has not previously experienced. Barking is also used when a dog is excited or wants attention.

1. When your dog is barking, you need to command and control it without giving the impression that you are joining in. This means that you need a new, sudden sound to shock your dog into silence. The ideal mechanism is very simple—a few pebbles in a tin can. While your dog is barking, vigrously rattle the tin.

2. Stop rattling the can the instant your dog is quiet and turns toward you. You now have its attention. Calmly give the *quiet* command. Go to your dog to control it or call it to you. The problem will be controlled if you stay calm and do not join in with your dog.

3. As soon as your dog quietly comes to you, praise and reward it. Give the *quiet* command so your dog understands that it is being rewarded for not barking. Always keep the can handy. The size of the can and the number and size of pebbles can vary the intensity and tone.

what not to do

When your dog barks and bounces to the door, never run after it shouting "*Shut up!*" If you make more noise, your dog will get even more excited because it thinks that it now has the pack joining in. The louder you shout, the more your dog thinks that you are backing it up and the more it will bark.

● see: feedback, p. 38 and learning to bark on command, p. 93

 GOLD You remain calm when there are noises that excite your dog into barking. Your dog is quiet on command. When you go to the door, you can control your dog by having it on its leash with you.

 SILVER You do not shout and run after your dog, but remain calm. When your dog starts to bark, it responds to the rattle of the can. It is then quiet while you praise and control it.

 BRONZE You do not shout or run after your dog. You are becoming much calmer in the handling of your dog. Your dog comes to you to be rewarded, but you need to put it on its leash and confine it before opening the door.

commands used

- *b e d*
  Use a positive tone.
- *d o w n*

problem solving

4:3

begging at the table

You cannot regulate your dog's diet if it is being given scraps of food all day. Much of what we eat is very bad for a dog's health. It is in the best interest of the dog to train it to go to its bed and to keep it away from the table during meals. Feed it only from its own bowl.

2. Place your dog's bowl near its bed. When you are about to eat, show your dog that you have put a treat in its bowl. Send your dog to its bed and bowl using the *b e d* command. Let it eat the treat from the bowl, then command it *d o w n* onto its bed.

1. Your dog looks to you as its provider of food. It naturally follows that if your dog sees you eating, it will assume that if it's good for you then it must be good for it, too. Your dog will come closer and closer, hoping that a scrap may fall within its reach.

3. Teach your dog to remain on its bed. Release it when you have finished eating. Gradually, the begging will stop, as there is no incentive to continue. When your dog has reached this stage, drop step 2. Any scraps should be put in its bowl away from the table.

what not to do

Never feed your dog from the table; this won't satisfy it and make it go away. It will salivate, whine, and bark for more. If you give your dog a scrap of food from your plate once or twice, your dog will anticipate that it is going to join you every time you are eating.

- see: learning to go to bed, p. 75

GOLD Your dog goes to its bed when you eat. Your dog doesn't bother you at meal times.

SILVER You dog is learning to stay by its bowl away from the table while you are eating. You have to take your dog to its bed and recommand it to remain in its bed while you are eating.

BRONZE Your dog begs at the table and demands food. To control it, you can put your dog into the *d o w n* by your chair so that it learns to remain still while you are eating. It receives no food from the table and only gets food in its own bowl.

car sickness

Traveling by car is part of modern life, but some dogs, like some people, suffer from motion sickness. If your pup suffers genuine motion sickness, medication can be obtained from your veterinarian. Fear and anxiety about the movement of the car, however, are at the root of most adverse reactions shown by pups. A combination of calming medication and training will solve the problem.

1. Make the car an enjoyable place to be. Put your pup's bed and some toys in the car, creating a familiar, pleasant environment. Put your pup into the car at various times during the day, perhaps even while you are cleaning it. Stay close to the pup and praise and reassure it.

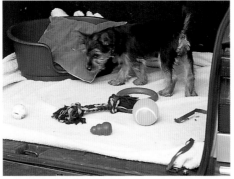

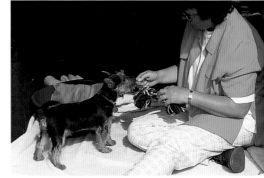

2. It takes time and patience to make your pup feel comfortable in the car. Another thing you can do to make the experience more enjoyable is to feed your dog there. Occasionally, close the doors for a few seconds. Then open them up, praise the pup, and take it out of the car.

3. Spend some time sitting with your pup in the backseat and playing with it. Other times, play in the front seat. Occasionally, start up the engine. When your pup is relaxed about this, ask someone to sit with the pup in the car while you drive a short distance. If the pup is relaxed, gradually increase the distance.

what not to do

Never simply put a pup into a car, especially if it is too small to brace itself against the changing movements. A pup needs to become acclimatized to a car and its motion. Your pup's first experiences should be as uneventful and pleasant as you can make them.

• see: picking up your pup, p. 24 (steps 1 and 2) and traveling in the car, p. 47

 GOLD Your pup travels in the car without suffering motion sickness. You are careful never to brake suddenly or make hard turns.

 SILVER Your pup travels short journeys without suffering motion sickness. Your pup travels better if someone sits close to it. You have to restrict your pup's view so that it isn't frightened by moving traffic. You should drive more carefully.

 BRONZE Your pup salivates and occasionally vomits in the car. Even on short journeys you have to stop and take your pup for a short walk before returning home. You should drive more carefully.

4:5

aggression over food or a toy

Any form of aggression should not be taken lightly, whether in a puppy or an adult dog. Aggression can be caused by fear, pain, resentment at feeling dominated, or possessiveness. It is also associated with the sex drive. Obedience and agility training, however, can build your dog's confidence and resolve its aggression. Teach your pup to accept your handling, including having its mouth opened.

1• To prevent aggression while your pup is feeding, stay close to it when you put its food down. Whenever you give your pup anything edible, train the pup to get used to your presence while it is eating. This teaches it that you are there to give it more food, not to take it away.

what not to do

Sometimes it is necessary to remove your dog's food or toy if it is overly possessive. Do not aggravate the situation by putting it on its guard; offer it a piece of food or something more interesting to divert its attention.

- see: playing, pp. 26–27; positions, p. 31; and retrieving, p. 62 (steps 1-6)

2• Hold two bowls of food and give one to the pup. When it has finished, give it the second bowl by picking up the first bowl and putting down the second in exchange. It requires expert timing and handling to understand your pup's reaction and read its different signals.

GOLD — Your dog allows you to take food and toys from it.

SILVER — Your dog shows no aggression when it is eating and allows you to take food and toys from it by exchange.

BRONZE — Your dog shows no aggression when it is eating. Your dog is aggressive over its toys. You need to train your dog to respect your handling. Teach it the *d o w n* position and to hold and release articles on command.

aggression toward people

Whatever type of aggression your dog shows, it is important to understand the circumstances that cause it; it is impossible to create a training program if the behavior seems unpredictable. Obtain your veterinarian's advice before beginning any remedial action. If there is a psychological reason for the behavior, drug therapy may be helpful.

1. In some cases, to control the dog and protect yourself, it is advisable to train it to wear a muzzle. As long as you know that the dog cannot cause any damage, you will have the confidence to control its aggression. The muzzle also allows your dog to mix safely with the family instead of being isolated, which could exacerbate the problem.

muzzle
to be used
during training

2. Preventive measures must be taken in any situation that brings your dog into contact with people in the home or outside. Build your dog's confidence in the presence of strangers, but don't force it to accept people. Allow it enough distance so that it doesn't feel threatened and become aggressive. Make your dog feel confident in your handling.

3. Diversion training draws your dog's attention away from what is troubling it. This enables you to build your dog's confidence with praise and rewards for showing tolerance and friendliness. Once you teach your dog to respond to a toy or food, you can use the item to divert its attention from the source of trouble.

the problem

Aggressive behavior toward people is one of the most worrying problems. This can be related to the dog's lack of socialization or individual attention. Your dog may fear a situation from which it cannot escape and defends itself by going on the attack. You can help by avoiding situations that you are unable to control.

- see: responding to its own name, p. 28; positions, pp. 30-31; grooming, pp. 32-33; feedback, p. 38; playing, p. 57; and examination, p. 91

 GOLD Your dog accepts being handled by any member of the family. Your dog shows no aggression to guests who come into the house. Your dog allows friendly strangers to approach it and will allow itself to be petted.

 SILVER Your dog accepts being handled by any member of the family. Your dog is not friendly toward strangers. You need to socialize your dog in a controlled environment such as a Dog Training Class, with advice from experienced instructors.

 BRONZE Your dog shows aggressive tendencies. First contact the veterinarian—your dog may have a health problem. Start to teach your dog to go into the *down* position on command.

4:7

facing new situations

A dog must be exposed to a variety of potentially fearful situations that may occur in its everyday life in order to give it the confidence to accept them. Whether it is learning to accept people, animals, or new situations, you need to give it confidence. A dog is often aggressive because it is afraid.

1. Put your dog on its leash. Hold the leash by the handle and allow your dog to go ahead and investigate. Talk quietly, and don't make any sudden movement that could frighten it. Keep at a distance so that it relaxes. When introducing a new experience, go slowly and work within your dog's ability until it no longer shows resentment.

2. As your dog gains confidence, gradually expose it to the situation that created its fear. Keep your dog on a leash and talk quietly to keep it relaxed. Some forms of aggression, especially those directed at humans, can be too dangerous for an inexperienced handler and you should seek professional advice. An extremely vicious dog that cannot be professionally retrained may need to be painlessly destroyed.

what not to do

Don't have your dog off the leash in a new situation; it is likely to run away or circle around other animals, barking aggressively. When trying to control a situation, do not become hostile. Remember that aggression leads to aggression. When your dog is on leash, keep at a distance so that it gains confidence and learns not to be afraid.

• see: feedback, pp. 38-39; playing, p. 57; and examination, p. 91

GOLD Your dog has confidence in you and your handling. Your dog accepts new situations. You can control your dog with the "*N o !*" command and attract its attention by using its name.

SILVER You can take your dog into new situations and control it on the leash. Your dog remains still on command and does not react with fear or aggression. You are building your dog's confidence with obedience training.

BRONZE Your dog shows aggressive tendencies. You need to build your dog's confidence with some obedience training and obtain advice from a trainer who has expertise in behavioral problems.

stealing things
and running away with them

Your dog has no sense of value. A silk scarf or your best shoes are the same as its favorite rag or chewy toy. The real value for your dog lies in your reaction when it picks up certain objects. Your dog may steal various articles in order to attract your attention and will enjoy prolonging the game by running away with you following in hot pursuit.

1. Keep calm and never show agitation if you see that your dog is going to pick up something that it shouldn't. First try to ignore it. Your dog's interest will be measured in the amount of attention you give it. You can help the situation by putting things away and keeping temptation out of reach.

2. If your dog starts to run away, pick up one of its toys or a treat and pretend that it is an extremely exciting and interesting thing. Lure your dog to you; don't command it. Get the dog close enough to you to exchange the articles. Play a game, making its toys more interesting.

what not to do

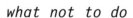

If your dog picks up something that it shouldn't, never get excited and chase it when it runs away. Otherwise, your dog will steal various articles that it shouldn't because you have given it your attention. You will accidentally teach your dog that a game will develop if it picks up certain articles.

* see: playing, pp. 26-27, 56; recalling the puppy to you, pp. 36-37; and retrieving, pp. 44-46

 GOLD Your dog doesn't run away with things. If your dog picks up something that it shouldn't, you can control it by keeping calm, then encouraging it to come to you and exchanging the article for something that it is allowed to have.

 SILVER Your dog picks up articles that it shouldn't, trying to get you to play with it. Your pup will come to you to exchange the article for a tasty food treat.

 BRONZE Your dog picks up things and runs away with them. Keep calm and divert its attention onto its dinner or something that it is allowed to have. Don't chase after your dog, even in play. Teach it to chase you.

problem solving

4:9

refusing to come when called

Your dog may not come when called because it has learned the wrong association with your command. You may have commanded it to come to you while it was running away or while it was playing with another dog; now your command is associated with just that. However tempting it may be, never call your dog to you in order to tell it off.

SINGLE-TONE WHISTLES

horn with individual tone

plastic with specific tone

what not to do

Don't command your dog to come when it is running away from you; after only a couple of occasions, it will be conditioned to the wrong association. Always time the command with the action you want—this is critical to your dog's understanding. Gain its attention by using its name before giving the command.

- see: responding to its own name, p. 28; recalling the puppy to you, pp. 36-37; playing hide-and-seek, p. 56; and recall to heel, p. 87

retraining correct association

To retrain your dog, introduce a new command or a different signal, such as a whistle. (A single-tone whistle sounds the same at a distance and is not influenced by your mood or the environment.)

2. As soon as your dog turns to you, loosen the leash. Move backward, encouraging your dog to come by using your new command or giving several short blasts on your whistle. As your dog moves toward you, gather up the leash, praise it, and give your command, saying "*Good dog. Come.*"

1. Choose an area with few distractions. Put your dog on its leash and walk forward; keep the leash loose and stay quiet. After about ten paces, stop. Keep quiet as you stop and loosen the leash so that your dog can continue to walk forward toward the end of the leash. As your dog reaches the end, call its name and simultaneously tug the leash.

3. As soon as your dog makes contact with you, be ready with praise and a reward. Whenever your dog comes to you, make it memorable, inspiring it to come when called, whatever else is happening. Repeat this until your dog instantly responds to its name and happily comes to you.

- *release*
- *OK — away you go!*
- *come*
- *recall*

drag line with a snap

training in open spaces

1. You need to extend your control to the outside to develop this training. For this, you need a long drag line that is light enough for your dog to drag along as it runs. Take your dog on its leash to a safe area. Place your dog on a fixed collar and exchange the leash for the line.

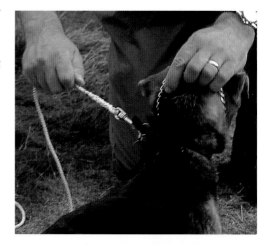

2. Let your dog go, giving the *release* command and hand signal, saying *"OK — away you go!"* Make sure the line is not entangled while it is dragged along by your dog. Allow your dog to go some distance but always maintain control. Stay within easy reach of the line.

4. The instant your dog looks up, encourage it to come to you. As it moves toward you of its own will, drop the line but remain standing on it as a precaution. Continue encouraging your dog to come to you. If it is slow to come, turn and run away. Continue with the line-training until your dog instantly responds.

3. After your dog has had a short run and while it is facing away from you, perhaps investigating something, step on the line. Then pick up the line and call your dog's name, followed by the *come* command or a long blast on your whistle. If your dog takes no notice, repeat its name or blow the whistle again and at the same time give a sharp tug on the line.

 GOLD You can attract your dog's attention at a distance. You can let your dog have a free run and it comes back to you on command.

5. Make a big fuss and reward your dog. After a few seconds, let it go again. Give the *recall* command only when you have your dog's attention and you are sure to get the correct response. Dogs rarely run away—they run toward something that is more interesting or fun than you are.

 SILVER You can let your dog run free as long as there are no distractions. Your dog can exercise with the drag line and comes to you when called. You and your dog need to train in and around controlled distractions such as a Dog Training Class.

 BRONZE Your dog won't come when it is called and goes away sniffing and hunting, returning only when it feels like it. Teach your dog to play with you and make it fun for it to respond to you. Enroll in a Dog Training Class to obtain advice while you are training.

4:10

chasing bicyclists, joggers, or livestock

All dogs possess the instinct to chase. When a dog hunts its prey in the wild, the chase is the most exciting part. The tricky problem with chasing bicyclists or joggers is that each time they get away, the desire to chase is reinforced because your dog thinks it has successfully chased them off its territory. Your dog needs to be reconditioned around movement and praised for good behavior.

1. When your dog chases a bicyclist, go to your dog and get it under control, putting it back on its leash. Whenever you are out walking your dog on its leash, anticipate anything that it is likely to chase. Don't delay getting it under control.

2. Put your dog in the *sit* and bring its collar high on its neck, allowing a couple of inches of leash to give you optimum control. Ask an assistant to ride by on a bicycle and as soon as your dog shows the slightest interest, command "*No!*" or "*Leave!*" Distract your dog with a toy or by playing.

the problem

Chasing must be turned into an unpleasant pastime. The best remedy for this behavior is to set up a situation. Ask an assistant to ride by on a bicycle. As your dog runs alongside the bike, have your assistant give it a shock, by either making a nasty sound or by throwing something toward it. Do not hit the dog with the object.

- see: feedback, pp. 36–37; playing, p. 57; and stop or drop on command at a distance, pp. 100–101

retraining to stock

Never take any risks when you are around livestock, even with the most highly trained dog. With a known chaser, keep it on its leash and be ready to control and discipline it. If it shows the slightest interest, say "*No!*" in a stern voice. If it makes any attempt to chase, tug hard on its collar.

 GOLD You can control your dog at a distance. It stops on command of *sit* or *down* and you can call it back to you. Your dog correctly responds when you say "*No!*" and stops when there are possible distractions that it could chase. Your dog waits for you to approach it and put it back on its leash.

 SILVER You have to put your dog on its leash when there are joggers or bicyclists around. When it is on its leash, it makes no attempt to chase and correctly responds when you say "*No!*" Your dog remains in the *sit* while the distractions go past.

 BRONZE Your dog pulls and tries to chase things even while it is on its leash. You can keep your dog in the *sit* on a short leash and it will correctly respond when you say "*No!*" if you are some distance from the distraction.

4:11 problem solving

pulling on the leash

Dogs pull on the leash for several reasons. They may be excited about going for a walk, they may be competing with you or with other dogs being walked—they feel the need to be the leader of the pack. This problem can be solved by retraining your dog with better handling and teaching it to respect and understand a new command.

1. If your dog is pulling on the leash, try using a collar that fits better, such as a semi-slip collar, which is comfortable and adjustable. Bring the collar up high on the dog's neck to prevent it from throwing its weight against it. The collar should be loose, however, when your dog is close to your left side.

2. Hold the leash so that the collar is loose. The instant your dog moves forward, say "*No!*" and give a sharp tug. As your dog takes up the *heel*, praise it and give the *heel* command in an encouraging tone. Make sure your timing is accurate when correcting your dog.

3. If you find it difficult to teach your dog to walk to heel, or you have to walk two or more dogs, use a controlling head collar. The head collar acts as a bridle to control the head and prevents your dog from pulling. Eventually this creates the correct habit.

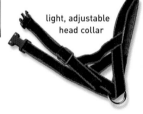

light, adjustable head collar

the problem

If the dog's collar is resting low on its neck, when it pulls it can throw its whole body weight forward and take most of the strain on its shoulders. With the leash wrapped around your wrist and your arm at full stretch, you find yourself being dragged along. Walking your dog becomes very uncomfortable. [Full-slip collars and leashes should only be used under the direction of an experienced Dog Trainer or Instructor.]

• see: feedback, pp. 38-39; walking to heel, p. 43; and heelwork, pp. 50-53, p. 84

GOLD Your dog walks on a loose leash by your side. Your dog responds to the *heel* command and walks on a loose leash.

SILVER When you go out, your dog initially pulls. Your dog responds to the collar being set high on its neck and walks on a loose leash, staying by your side when you hold the leash with both hands.

BRONZE Your dog continually pulls with just a collar and you have to use a head collar to walk it.

problem solving

4:12
play-biting

Play-biting is part of growing up. Puppies try to learn how hard they can bite before causing any damage. A pup's teeth are like needles and it must learn that games will stop even when light pressure is applied. Once the pup has its full strength and its adult teeth, it will know how not to cause harm during play if it has been properly trained.

1. If your pup starts to play-bite, give it something else to think about. Or, divert its attention onto something that it is allowed to bite, like a favorite chewy toy.

2. Always handle your pup in a very calm manner. Use your hands to control your pup by gently petting it and quietly talking to it. Use this physical attention to calm your pup. Teach children to handle a pup in a quiet way or use toys to divert its attention from biting.

3. If the pup persists, say *"N o !"* in a sharp, low growl. Never shout—use a strong tone, not a loud volume, and don't nag. Bring a hand under the lower jaw to help the pup close its mouth. The instant the pup stops, praise it in a gentle tone to calm and reassure it.

what not to do

Never tease your pup and don't play games that cause your pup to become aggressively excited. Children should be taught to keep calm and not to run around shouting and waving their arms when playing with their pup because the pup will play the only way it can—with its teeth. Never allow children to give a pup any form of correction.

• see: playing, pp. 26-27; responding to its own name, p. 28; and feedback, pp. 38-39

GOLD Your pup stops biting when you say *"N o !"* You can divert its attention onto its toys. Your pup stops biting when you handle it in a calm manner.

SILVER Your pup responds sometimes when you say *"N o !"* if it is not too excited. You can control your pup's biting if you stop any games and handle it in a calm manner.

BRONZE Your pup is easily excited and you need to handle it in a calm manner until it grows up. Don't keep nagging the pup to stop it from play-biting. Divert its attention with toys.

overexcitement

Dogs can get excited to the point of being out of control, especially when they are about to go outside. You need to desensitize your dog to anything that makes it uncontrollably excited. You must handle and control your dog in a calm, quiet manner and never shout or get excited yourself.

1. Going out should be a pleasure, not a nightmare. The excitement of getting out of the car must be controlled for the safety of your dog and others. Retrain your dog to get used to wearing its collar and leash by putting them on the dog in and around the house for a few seconds when you are not going out.

2. When going into any situation that could cause your dog to get excited, you must get control of it first. Make a habit of using your dog's collar and leash to get and keep control of your dog. Always put your dog on its leash before taking it out. Keep your voice and handling calm.

what not to do

When your dog gets excited at times other than when you are playing, it is important that it is not inadvertently encouraged by your own animated handling and shouted commands. Your dog is not deaf. Your job is to train it how to behave.

• see: discouraging running through a gate or door, p. 42 and heelwork, p. 52

GOLD Your dog responds to your calm control and handling. Your dog sits while its collar and leash are put on and walks out of the house under control. Your dog waits for its leash to be put on before getting out of the car.

SILVER You are able to control your dog's excitability with quiet, calm commands and nonexcited handling. It is learning to sit and have its collar and leash put on at times other than when going for a walk. It waits for its leash to be put on before getting out of the car.

BRONZE You can control your dog on its leash when guests visit. Your dog still gets excited about going out and you need to train it to have its collar and leash put on at other times during the day. The family must learn to handle and control it in a calm and nonexcited manner.

problem solving # 4:14

excessive sexual activity

Many pups show signs of sexual activity when playing or when they get excited. Sometimes they take out their frustration on a cushion or your leg. You need to divert the pup's attention or remove it so that the behavior doesn't become obsessive, especially around children.

1● Your pup doesn't deserve any physical or verbal abuse for this behavior. Go to your pup to control it. Take it by its collar and say *"No!"*; then remove it from the situation. Don't nag it.

the problem

The desire for sexual activity occurs in a pup during its development and in practically all intact males and females at some time in their adult life. Because this natural drive has a tendency to supersede all learned behavior, you need to control and prevent it from becoming obsessive.

● see: responding to its own name, p. 28; feedback, pp. 38-39; and playing, p. 57

2● Keep hold of your pup or put it on its leash until it has calmed down. Then, using nonexcited tones, reduce its sexual excitability. You need to be attentive to your pup's moods; as soon as you see your pup starting to use its front paws to take hold, say *"No!"* to command and divert it.

 GOLD As soon as you see your pup showing unwanted signs of sexual activity, you can divert it by saying *"No!"* and giving it a toy to play with.

 SILVER You have to put your pup on its leash to control it. You can divert its attention with some exercise or by making it go into the *down* position.

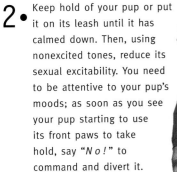

3● Once your pup has relaxed and calmed down, channel its energy into something else—either some formal training that requires its full concentration or onto a physical game under your control. If you see that it is going to run after another pup, put it back on its leash.

 BRONZE Your pup is easily excited, jumps on other pups, and tries to mount your leg and cushions. Get veterinary advice about hormone treatment or neutering.

4:15 | problem solving

submissive urination

A shy or nervous dog will suffer from submissive urination if it feels excessively dominated, if it is given certain forms of punishment, or if it feels that it is at the bottom of the pack. This type of dog lacks confidence and behaves in this way because it feels that it must make homage to everyone it encounters. You must restore its confidence.

1. Your dog comes to you in a low stance. Because it looks worried, you try harder to encourage it, often using eye contact. In dog language, however, this is a form of dominance. As you go to physically praise it, it stoops even lower or rolls over.

2. Consciously try to counteract your dog's submissive nature. Avoid making any sounds of frustration or annoyance when it shows signs of submission. Divert your eye contact. Stoop down to greet it instead of petting it from above. Let the dog jump up, which is an act of dominance by the dog.

3. Don't sympathize with a submissive dog like this; instead, distract it out of itself. While praising it, take hold of its collar so your dog can be placed on the ground in the *sit* or *stand*, and let it go. Let your dog take the initiative with guests.

what not to do

As you bend over your dog— something it perceives as a dominant posture— it rolls over in total submission and urinates. You either continue to praise this performance or become annoyed because it has urinated all over you or the carpet. This causes your dog to become even more worried, reinforcing the submissive urination problem.

- see: positions, pp. 29-30; recalling the puppy to you, p. 37; playing, p. 55; and jumping, p. 102

GOLD Your dog comes to you with confidence. You can praise your dog and it remains upright. You are training your dog to sit and accept praise from guests.

SILVER You allow your dog to come to you and jump up. You can praise and control your dog on four feet without it rolling over. You are teaching guests not to stare at the dog and to ignore it if it approaches in a low stance.

BRONZE Your dog lacks confidence. Ignore it when it occasionally rolls on its back. Let it jump up and quietly praise it. When you control it onto all fours, be ready with a treat to reward it in the *sit* or *stand*.

problem solving

4:16

chewing furniture

It is natural for puppies to chew things—it is a way of exploring their environment. They chew mainly when their second teeth are coming through, at about the age of 4 to 6 months. Puppies should be given one or two chewable objects as substitutes to distract the pup from chewing things that it shouldn't.

2. Quietly approach your pup; while it is engrossed, clap your hands in its ear and say "*N o !*" The shock will stop the pup in its tracks. Don't keep nagging. Get hold of the pup by the collar and take the object away. If you see the pup moving toward the object it wants to chew, say "*N o !*" and divert its attention onto something that it is allowed to chew.

1. Left on their own, pups and older dogs can become destructive. They are pack animals and dislike isolation. Pups recently taken from their mother and siblings often try to escape by digging and chewing, and they will cry and howl for attention. They often chew and dig in areas where your scent is strongest.

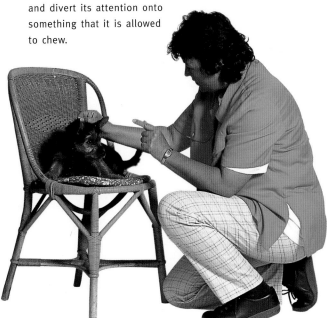

what not to do

All too often, when your pup hears your approach, it stops in anticipation of your company and it is too late for any correction. Don't go toward your pup in a menacing and threatening way. You may feel better after venting your anger, but the only thing that achieves is to teach your pup to fear you.

● see: feedback, pp. 38-39 and learning to be left alone, p. 71

GOLD
When your pup is left alone it does not chew on things it shouldn't. You can control your pup if you see that it is about to start to chew the furniture and divert it onto something it can have.

SILVER
You can leave your pup as long as it has something to occupy it, like a new toy or a large rawhide to chew on, and it is confined to an area where there is no furniture to chew.

BRONZE
Your pup will chew the furniture if it is not supervised. Don't leave your pup in a position to get into trouble.

4:17

separation anxiety

Between 8 to 12 weeks of age, a pup should not have any fearful experiences. Being left alone often causes anxiety, and if left for long enough, the pup will try to escape. If you leave your pup often, this behavior will become ingrained and you will have a dog that can never be left without destroying its surroundings.

the problem

The desire to escape from isolation is natural behavior and should not be punished. It will take time to build up the dog's confidence. It may feel unnatural to you, but pay less attention to your dog— don't make a big fuss when leaving or returning. Don't let it constantly follow you around.

• see: learning to be left alone, p. 71; learning to go to bed, p. 75; and positions out of sight, p. 90

comfort blanket and toy

When leaving, keep things matter-of-fact, give your dog an article of your recently worn clothing or a novel toy. Calmly say "*Goodbye*." Then leave the dog for a few seconds. Gradually increase the time that you stay away. Don't make a fuss when you return. You may have to get a dogsitter until your dog overcomes its fear.

cage training

If you force your dog into the cage, it will immediately cry to be let out. To get your dog used to the cage, start by having the cage close to you until your dog settles in it. Gradually move further away from the cage until you are out of sight. Very slowly increase the time that your dog spends in the cage.

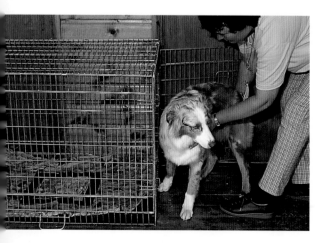

 GOLD You can leave your dog (with the radio on) by itself without it becoming upset. Your dog doesn't jump up and scratch the door. On return, your dog is calm and can accept praise without becoming overexcited.

 SILVER You can leave your dog by itself and go to other rooms in the house. On your return, your dog is relaxed and does not jump up and get excited. Your dog is starting to understand the *quiet* command and does not follow you.

 BRONZE You are starting to build up a procedure when leaving and you can go to other rooms for a few seconds. Your dog is relaxed if it can hear your voice. You are learning to give less attention to your dog when you leave and return.

training score card

training exercise	number	date started	notes	date achieved

photocopy as many sheets as you need to record your dog's progress

index

acknowledgments

Quarto Publishing would like to acknowledge and thank the sources given below for pictures appearing on the following pages:

Jane Burton/Warren Photographic: title page, contents page, 6-7, 10tl, 11tr, 12tl, 14t & br, 15tr & b, 16br, 22-23, 48-49, 76-77, 104-105.

Key: t = top r = right l = left b = bottom

All other photographs are the copyright of Quarto Publishing

Quarto Publishing and Jacqui O'Brien would like to thank the following owners/handlers and dogs for helping with this book:

My own dogs Rhumba and Chazz; Dennis Bell with Amy and Zara; Jenni Brown with Buster; Karen Cato with Daisey, Ben, and Dash; Philip Cook with Teaka and Kuma; Cayley Dawson with Hetty; Barbara Gell with Cara; Denise and Robert Hunt with Emma, Barney, and Tonto; Jill Lamin with Amber and Beau; Rita Musk with Piper; Helen Rogers with Maisie; Michael Stewart with Ben and Trixie; Lorraine Turnbull with Molly; Cathy While with Gizmo; Mr. and Mrs. Pullman with Twiglet and Go; Mrs. P. Raegan and Jack; Mr. J. Randall and Ember; Mr. and Mrs. Thatcher and Xhosa.

Special thanks to Grant Wienand, Joel Veterinary Clinic, Joel Street Farm, Eastcote, Middx. HA5 2PD and Pet Fayre, 6 Main Parade, Chorleywood, Herts WD3 5RB for supplying training toys and equipment.